# 1 Workplace Plus

## Living and Working in English

**Joan Saslow**

**Tim Collins**

### Regional Consultant Board

**Edwina Hoffman**
Series Advisor

Longman

**Workplace Plus with Grammar Booster 1: Living and Working in English**

Pearson Education, 10 Bank Street, White Plains, NY 10606

Vice president, director of publishing: Allen Ascher
Senior acquisitions editor: Marian Wassner
Senior development editor: Marcia Schonzeit
Assistant editor: Patricia Lattanzio
Vice president, director of design and production: Rhea Banker
Executive managing editor: Linda Moser
Senior production editor: Christine Lauricella
Production supervisor: Liza Pleva
Senior manufacturing manager: Patrice Fraccio
Manufacturing supervisor: Dave Dickey
Cover design: Ann France
Text design: Ann France
Text composition: Word and Image
Illustrations: Craig Attebery, pp. 36, 37, 45, 46, 61, 74, 81, 82, 110; Crowleart Group, pp. 63, 80, 82, 91, 92, 114, 128-130; Brian Hughes, pp. 1, 4, 26, 27, 31, 33, 34, 36, 38, 39, 41, 43, 46, 48, 49, 50, 51, 56, 58, 60, 70, 73, 75, 79, 87, 97, 108-111, 117, 121; Paul McCusker, pp. 27, 68, 80, 105, 111; Suzanne Mogensen, pp. 2, 15, 20, 25, 33, 40, 52, 53, 62, 66, 86, 88, 91, 100, 114; Tom Newsom, pp. 48, 51, 54, 111; Dusan Petricic, p. 101; Stephen Quinlan, p. 99; NSV Productions, pp. 13, 16, 22, 24, 38, 40, 46, 49, 85, 89, 106, 120, 142; Meryl Treatner, pp. 12, 25, 30, 42, 72, 75, 84, 85, 90, 96, 97, 102, 120, 126; Word & Image Design, pp. 5, 13, 19, 20, 21, 32, 33, 44, 45, 55-58, 61, 68, 69, 70, 73, 81, 82, 89, 93, 94, 104-106, 116-118, 129; Anna Veltfort, pp. 17, 18, 23, 29, 35, 41, 47, 53, 59, 65, 71, 77, 78, 83, 87, 95, 101, 107, 113, 119, 125, 131
Photography: Gilbert Duclos, pp. 2, 3, 6-11, 14, 15, 19, 21, 26, 27, 31, 38, 39, 43, 45, 50, 51, 55, 56, 57, 61, 62, 63, 67, 69, 73, 74, 75, 79, 86, 87, 89, 91, 92, 97, 98, 99, 103, 110, 111, 115, 117, 122, 123, 127, 128; Page 21 © (tl) Juan Monino/Et/Getty Images, (ml) PathDoc/Shutterstock, (mr) TMI/Alamy, (bl) Portra Images/Digital Vision/Getty Images, (br)Ruslan Kudrin/Shutterstock; page 32 Chronis Jons/Stone; page 85 © J. Henley/First Light
Grammar Booster: Craig Attebery, p.GB-7; Crowleart Group, p.GB-13; Dennis Dzielak, p. GB-14; Brian Hughes, pp. GB-6, GB-7, GB-12, BG-16, GB-26, GB-29; Andy Myer, pp. GB-10, GB-11; NSV Productions, pp. GB-1; GB=3, GB-20; Don Stewart, pp. GB-19, GB-24; Meryl Treatner, pp. GB-14, GB-17, GB-22, GB-24, GB-26; Chris Vallo, p. GB-6

**Library of Congress Cataloging-in-Publication Data**

ISBN: 0-13-192799-X

| LONGMAN ON THE WEB |
| --- |
| Longman.com offers online resources for teachers and students. Access our Companion Websites, our online catalog, and our local offices around the world. |
| Visit us at longman.com. |

11 12 13 12 15—V064—15 14

# Contents

# Correlations[1]

| Unit | Correlations to National Standards | | | Correlations to State Standards | |
|---|---|---|---|---|---|
| | SCANS Competencies | CASAS Life Skill Competencies | EFF Content Standards | Florida | Texas |
| **1** **Your life and work** page 12 | • Understands social systems • Acquires and evaluates information • Interprets and communicates information • Works well with people of culturally diverse backgrounds | 0.1.2, 0.1.4, 0.2.2, 0.2.4, 4.1.1, 4.1.2, 4.1.3, 4.1.6, 4.1.7, 4.1.8, 4.1.9, 4.2.4, 4.3.2, 4.4.1, 4.4.2, 4.4.5, 4.4.6, 4.6.1, 4.6.2, 4.6.3, 4.7.1, 4.7.2, 4.8.1, 4.8.2, 4.8.5, 4.8.6, 4.9.1, 4.9.3 | A full range of EFF Content Standards is included in this unit. The following are emphasized: • Read with Understanding 1–4 • Convey Ideas in Writing 3, 4 • Speak So Others Can Understand 1–4 • Listen Actively 1–4 • Take Responsibility for Learning 1–3, 6 | Student's Book: 18.01, 18.02, 19.01, 19.02, 19.03, 20.01, 20.02, 32.02, 32.04, 33.02, 33.03  Workbook: 18.02, 19.01, 19.02, 19.03, 20.01, 20.02, 22.01, 22.02, 32.05, 33.01, 33.02 | Student's Book: 18.01, 18.02, 19.01, 19.02, 19.03, 20.01, 20.02, 32.02, 32.04, 33.02, 33.03  Workbook: 18.02, 19.01, 19.02, 19.03, 20.01, 20.02, 22.01, 22.02, 32.05, 33.01, 33.02 |
| **2** **Your environment** page 24 | • Understands social and organizational systems • Acquires and evaluates information • Interprets and communicates information | 0.1.2, 0.1.3, 0.1.5, 0.2.3, 0.2.4, 1.1.3, 1.3.7, 1.9.4, 1.9.6, 2.2.1, 2.2.5, 2.5.2, 2.5.3, 2.5.4, 2.6.1, 5.6.1, 5.6.4 | A full range of EFF Content Standards is included in this unit. The following are emphasized: • Read with Understanding 1–4 • Speak So Others Can Understand 1–4 • Listen Actively 1–4 • Observe Critically 1–5 • Advocate and Influence 1-5 | Student's Book: 18.01, 29.01, 32.02, 32.04, 33.02, 33.03, 33.04, 33.05  Workbook: 18.01, 29.01, 32.03, 32.05, 33.01, 33.02, 33.04, 33.05 | Student's Book: 18.01, 29.01, 32.02, 32.04, 33.02, 33.03, 33.04, 33.05  Workbook: 18.01, 29.01, 32.05, 33.01, 33.02, 33.04, 33.05 |
| **3** **Your equipment and machines** page 36 | • Uses technology • Acquires and evaluates information • Interprets and communicates information | 0.1.2, 0.1.3, 0.1.5, 0.2.3, 0.2.4, 1.4.1, 1.7.3, 1.7.4, 1.7.5, 2.1.6, 2.1.8, 4.3.1, 4.3.3, 4.4.3, 4.4.8, 4.5.1, 4.5.4, 4.5.5, 4.5.6, 4.5.7, 4.9.4 | A full range of EFF Content Standards is included in this unit. The following are emphasized: • Observe Critically 1–5 • Solve Problems and Make Decisions 1–6 • Cooperate with Others 1–4 • Guide Others 1–4 • Take Responsibility for Learning 1–3, 5, 6 | Student's Book: 21.01, 23.02, 23.04, 32.02, 32.04, 33.02, 33.03  Workbook: 21.01, 23.02, 23.04, 32.03, 32.05 | Student's Book: 21.01, 23.02, 23.04, 32.02, 32.04, 33.02, 33.03  Workbook: 21.01, 23.02, 23.04, 32.05 |
| **4** **Your customers** page 48 | • Serves customers • Works toward agreement • Acquires and evaluates information • Interprets and communicates information | 0.1.2, 0.1.4, 0.1.5, 0.2.3, 0.2.4, 1.1.9, 1.2.1, 1.2.5, 1.3.1, 1.3.3, 1.3.7, 1.3.9, 1.6.3, 1.7.2, 4.8.3, 4.8.4, 4.8.5, 4.8.6, 7.3.1, 7.3.2, 8.1.2, 8.1.4 | A full range of EFF Content Standards is included in this unit. The following are emphasized: • Read with Understanding 1–4 • Convey Ideas in Writing 1–4 • Observe Critically 1–5 • Solve Problems and Make Decisions 1–6 • Advocate and Influence 1–5 • Guide Others 1–4 • Take Responsibility for Learning 1–3, 5, 6 | Student's Book: 22.03, 28.02, 28.03, 32.02, 32.04, 33.02, 33.03, 33.07  Workbook: 22.03, 28.02, 32.03, 32.05, 32.06, 33.02, 33.03 | Student's Book: 22.03, 28.02, 28.03, 32.02, 32.04, 33.02, 33.03, 33.07  Workbook: 22.03, 28.02, 32.05, 32.06, 33.01, 33.02, 33.03 |
| **5** **Your time** page 60 | • Allocates time • Acquires and evaluates information • Interprets and communicates information • Understands social and organizational systems | 0.1.2, 0.1.5, 0.2.3, 0.2.4, 2.1.3, 2.2.4, 2.3.1, 2.3.2, 2.6.2, 2.7.1, 3.1.2 | A full range of EFF Content Standards is included in this unit. The following are emphasized: • Convey Ideas in Writing 2–4 • Observe Critically 1–5 • Use Math to Solve Problems and Communicate 2, 3, 5 • Plan 1, 2, 4, 5 • Learn Through Research 1–3 | Student's Book: 25.01, 25.02, 25.03, 26.02, 32.02, 32.04, 33.02, 33.03, 33.07  Workbook: 25.01, 25.02, 25.03, 26.02, 32.03, 32.05 | Student's Book: 25.01, 25.02, 25.03, 26.02, 32.02, 32.04, 33.02, 33.03, 33.07  Workbook: 25.01, 25.02, 25.03, 26.02, 32.05 |

[1]Correlations are also available at **www.longman.com/correlations**.

| Unit | Correlations to National Standards | | | Correlations to State Standards | |
|------|------|------|------|------|------|
| | SCANS Competencies | CASAS Life Skill Competencies | EFF Content Standards | Florida | Texas |
| **Your Supplies and Resources** page 72 | • Allocates resources<br>• Understands organizational systems<br>• Participates as a member of a team<br>• Acquires and evaluates information<br>• Interprets and communicates information<br>• Serves customers<br>• Teaches others | 0.1.2, 0.1.5, 0.2.3, 0.2.4, 1.1.1, 1.1.6, 1.2.2, 1.2.5, 1.3.8, 1.6.1, 3.5.1, 3.5.2, 3.5.3 | A full range of EFF Content Standards is included in this unit. The following are emphasized:<br>• Convey Ideas in Writing 1–4<br>• Listen Actively 1–4<br>• Observe Critically 1–5<br>• Guide Others 1–3<br>• Take Responsibility for Learning 1–3, 5, 6 | Student's Book: 24.05, 28.01, 28.03, 32.01, 32.02, 32.04, 32.06, 33.02, 33.03, 33.05, 33.06<br><br>Workbook: 24.05, 28.01, 32.03, 32.05, 32.07, 33.06 | Student's Book: 24.05, 28.01, 28.03, 32.01, 32.02, 32.04, 32.06, 33.02, 33.03, 33.05, 33.06<br><br>Workbook: 24.05, 28.01, 32.05, 32.07, 33.06 |
| **Your Relationships** page 84 | • Understands social and organizational systems<br>• Acquires and evaluates information<br>• Interprets and communicates information<br>• Negotiates | 0.1.2, 0.1.5, 0.2.3, 0.2.4 | A full range of EFF Content Standards is included in this unit. The following are emphasized:<br>• Solve Problems and Make Decisions 1–3, 5, 6<br>• Plan 1–5<br>• Take Responsibility for Learning 1–3, 5, 6 | Student's Book: 22.03, 31.01, 32.02, 32.04, 33.02, 33.03, 33.07<br><br>Workbook: 22.03, 31.01, 32.03, 32.05, 32.06, 33.02 | Student's Book: 22.03, 31.01, 32.02, 32.04, 33.02, 33.03, 33.07<br><br>Workbook: 22.03, 31.01, 32.05, 32.06, 33.02 |
| **Your Health and Safety** page 96 | • Acquires and evaluates information<br>• Interprets and communicates information<br>• Understands social and organizational systems | 0.1.2, 0.1.5, 0.2.3, 0.2.4, 1.9.7, 2.1.2, 2.1.7, 2.1.8, 2.5.1, 2.5.2, 2.5.3, 3.1.1, 3.1.2, 3.1.3, 3.2.1, 3.3.1, 3.3.2, 3.3.3, 3.4.2, 3.4.3, 3.5.4, 4.3.2, 4.3.3, 4.3.4, 5.3.8 | A full range of EFF Content Standards is included in this unit. The following are emphasized:<br>• Convey Ideas in Writing 1–4<br>• Listen Actively 1–4<br>• Solve Problems and Make Decisions 1, 3, 4, 6<br>• Advocate and Influence 1–3, 5<br>• Take Responsibility for Learning 1–4, 6 | Student's Book: 23.01, 23.02, 23.04, 24.01, 24.02, 24.03, 25.04, 27.01, 32.02, 32.04, 32.05, 33.02, 33.03, 33.06<br><br>Workbook: 23.01, 23.02, 24.01, 24.02, 24.03, 25.04, 27.01, 32.03, 33.03, 33.08 | Student's Book: 23.01, 23.02, 23.04, 24.01, 24.02, 24.03, 25.04, 32.02, 32.04, 32.05, 33.02, 33.03<br><br>Workbook: 23.01, 23.02, 24.01, 24.02, 24.03, 25.04, 33.03, 33.08 |
| **Your Money** page 108 | • Allocates money<br>• Serves customers<br>• Acquires and evaluates information<br>• Interprets and communicates information | 0.1.2, 0.1.5, 0.2.3, 0.2.4, 1.1.6, 1.2.2, 1.2.3, 1.2.4, 1.2.5, 1.3.2, 1.3.3, 1.3.4, 1.3.6, 1.5.1, 1.5.2, 1.5.3, 1.8.1, 1.8.2, 1.8.3, 1.8.4, 1.8.5, 1.9.2, 2.5.7, 2.6.4, 4.2.1, 4.7.1, 5.4.2, 5.8.1, 5.8.2, 5.8.3, 6.0.1, 6.0.2, 6.0.3 | A full range of EFF Content Standards is included in this unit. The following are emphasized:<br>• Convey Ideas in Writing 1–4<br>• Speak So Others Can Understand 1–4<br>• Listen Actively 1–4<br>• Use Math to Solve Problems and Communicate 1–5 | Student's Book: 25.05, 25.06, 26.05, 32.02, 32.04, 33.02, 33.03, 33.07<br><br>Workbook: 25.05, 25.06, 26.05, 32.03, 32.05, 33.02 | Student's Book: 25.05, 25.06, 26.05, 32.02, 32.04, 33.02, 33.03, 33.07<br><br>Workbook: 25.05, 25.06, 26.05, 32.05, 33.02 |
| **Your Career** page 120 | • Acquires and evaluates information<br>• Interprets and communicates information | 0.1.2, 0.1.5, 0.2.3, 0.2.4, 4.1.2, 4.1.3, 4.1.4, 4.1.5, 4.1.6, 4.1.7, 4.2.4, 4.3.2, 4.4.1, 4.4.2, 4.4.4, 4.4.5, 4.4.6, 4.4.7, 4.4.8, 4.6.1, 4.6.2, 4.6.3, 4.6.4, 4.6.5, 4.7.1, 4.7.2, 4.7.3, 4.7.4, 4.8.1, 4.8.5, 4.8.6, 4.9.3, 4.9.4 | A full range of EFF Content Standards is included in this unit. The following are emphasized:<br>• Observe Critically 1–5<br>• Advocate and Influence 1–5<br>• Take Responsibility for Learning 1, 3, 4, 6 | Student's Book: 18.01, 18.02, 18.03, 18.06, 19.01, 19.02, 19.03, 20.01, 20.02, 32.02, 32.04, 32.05, 33.02, 33.03, 33.07<br><br>Workbook: 18.01, 18.02, 18.03, 18.06, 32.03, 32.05, 32.06, 33.02 | Student's Book: 18.01, 18.02, 18.03, 19.01, 19.02, 19.03, 20.01, 20.02, 32.02, 32.04, 32.05, 33.02, 33.03, 33.07<br><br>Workbook: 18.01, 18.02, 18.03, 32.05, 32.06, 33.02 |

# Scope and sequence

| Unit | Workplace Skills | Lifeskills | Grammar | Grammar Booster |
|---|---|---|---|---|
| **1** **Your life and work** page 12 Grammar Booster page GB-1 | • Provides name and occupation upon request • Makes introductions • Introduces self | • Asks for and gives name, occupation, and country of origin • Makes introductions • Introduces self | • The present tense of *be*, singular forms | • The verb *be*: statements with singular subjects • Contractions with the verb *be* • The verb *be*: *yes/no* questions and short answers • *A* and *an* |
| **2** **Your environ-ment** page 24 Grammar Booster page GB-4 | • Identifies workplaces and places at work • Understands and gives directions to a place | • Identifies places in the community • Understands and gives directions to a place | • The present tense of *be*, plural forms | • The verb *be*: statements with plural subjects • The verb *be*: *yes/no* questions and short answers • The verb *be*: information questions |
| **3** **Your equip-ment and machines** page 36 Grammar Booster page GB-6 | • Identifies common workplace machines • Understands and gives instructions for using machines • Uses and troubleshoots technology | • Identifies common home machines • Understands and gives instructions for using machines | • Suggestions with *Let's* • Imperatives | • Suggestions with *Let's* • Commands |
| **4** **Your customers** page 48 Grammar Booster page GB-7 | • Offers service • Responds to customer requests • Apologizes • Takes customer orders | • Talks about clothes, colors, and sizes • Asks for refunds and exchanges • Complains about merchandise • Fills out a merchandise return form | • The simple present tense • *This, that, these,* and *those* | • The simple present tense: affirmative statements • *Have:* statements • The simple present tense: negative statements • The simple present tense: *yes/no* questions and short answers • The simple present tense: information questions • *This, that, these,* and *those* |
| **5** **Your time** page 60 Grammar Booster page GB-11 | • Asks for and says times, days, and dates • Talks about when work starts and ends • Understands work schedules • Understands punctuality | • Asks for and gives times, days, and dates • Talks about opening and closing times | • Impersonal statements with *It's* • Questions with *What time* and *When* • Ordinal numbers | • *It's* for days, dates, and times • *In, on, at, from,* and *to* for telling time • Information questions about time |

| Social Language | Vocabulary | Civics/Culture Concepts | Math Concepts and Practical Math Skills | Critical Thinking Skills |
|---|---|---|---|---|
| How to exchange personal information express sympathy offer support | • Occupations | • Shake hands and make eye contact. (W)[1]<br>• Jobs are not determined by gender.<br>• It's OK to ask about another's occupation.<br>• Use first names in informal settings.<br>• Use titles and last names in "official" settings. | • Understand and write numerals 0-100 (W)[1]<br>• Understand and use numbers in addresses and telephone numbers (W)[1]<br>• Count and classify items in a list<br>• Conduct a poll/survey | • Reasoning (classifies) |
| How to clarify politely request directions initiate a conversation express thanks acknowledge thanks | • Workplaces<br>• Places at work<br>• Places in the community | • Be friendly and helpful to others at work.<br>• It's OK to ask strangers for directions.<br>• Assist strangers who ask for help. | • Interpret spatial relationships | • Reasoning (makes inferences) |
| How to express dismay clarify suggest a course of action ask for help agree to a request express lack of knowledge | • Common machines and machine parts<br>• Verbs for machine operation | • It's OK to say "I don't know."<br>• Help co-workers to solve problems.<br>• It's OK to ask co-workers for help.<br>• It's OK to tell a supervisor about a problem. | • Follow sequential instructions | • Reasoning (applies knowledge to new situations) |
| How to express likes and dislikes state wants and needs apologize accept an offer complain offer a tentative answer | • Clothing, sizes, and colors | • Salespeople expect to help customers.<br>• Apologize when unable to fulfill a request.<br>• Unsatisfactory merchandise can be returned.<br>• Keep receipts as proof of purchase.<br>• It's important to follow company policy. | • Understand numerical and relative sizes<br>• Read receipts and understand prices, discounts, sum of prices, tax, and total | • Decision-making (evaluates and chooses the best alternative) |
| How to express concern express approval express uncertainty say good-bye | • Times of day, months, days, and years | • It's important to be punctual.<br>• Plan activities to observe work and business schedules and hours. | • Tell time<br>• Understand and use cardinal and ordinal numbers in dates<br>• Interpret and compare schedules | • Reasoning (makes inferences and draws conclusions)<br>• Decision-making (evaluates and chooses the best alternative) |

[1]Welcome Unit

| Social Language | Vocabulary | Civics/Culture Concepts | Math Concepts and Practical Math Skills | Critical Thinking Skills |
|---|---|---|---|---|
| How to<br>• start a conversation<br>• respond to a greeting<br>• ask for additional information<br>• solicit an opinion<br>• agree and disagree | • Common foods and drinks<br>• Cooking verbs | • It's OK to ask people about their tastes.<br>• It's important to plan ahead. | • Understand quantities and containers<br>• Understand measurements in recipes<br>• Follow sequential directions<br>• Compare quantities in recipes with available supplies | • Decision-making (evaluates and chooses the best alternative)<br>• Reasoning (sequences, draws conclusions) |
| How to<br>• ask for and give reasons<br>• state an obligation<br>• give and accept excuses | • Family members<br>• Action verbs | • Apologize and give a reason when unable to do something.<br>• Express sympathy for another's misfortune.<br>• Be willing to help out when an employer is short-handed. | • Estimate time needed to accomplish tasks<br>• Use schedules to manage time and commitments<br>• Calculate when to request a personal day based on company policy | • Decision-making (evaluates and chooses the best alternative) |
| How to<br>• conduct a phone conversation<br>• accept an apology<br>• offer to call back later<br>• make an appointment<br>• express sympathy<br>• offer good wishes<br>• express appreciation | • Parts of the body<br>• Common illnesses and injuries | • Understand and use telephone etiquette.<br>• Express concern when someone is ill or hurt.<br>• It's a duty to call 911 in an emergency. | • Schedule appointments<br>• Express dates in numbers based on understanding of sequence | • Reasoning (makes inferences and draws conclusions) |
| How to<br>• ask for change<br>• offer to check something<br>• inquire about a price<br>• ask for time to consider a purchase<br>• agree to make a purchase | • Coin and bill names<br>• Forms of payment<br>• Payment verbs | • It's OK to ask about prices.<br>• I.D. is required when paying with a personal check.<br>• Businesses have the right to determine types of payment accepted. | • Understand values of U.S. currency<br>• Calculate combinations of coins and bills that equal a stated price or amount<br>• Make change<br>• State prices<br>• Interpret bills and receipts | • Knowing how to learn (takes notes) |
| How to<br>• convince<br>• clarify | • Occupations<br>• Employment skills | • Arrive on time for a job interview.<br>• Appropriate dress and grooming are essential in an interview.<br>• Address an interviewer by title and last name. | • Compare required work hours at potential jobs with hours of availability | • Reasoning (makes associations)<br>• Decision-making (evaluates and chooses the best alternative) |

# Acknowledgments

The authors wish to acknowledge with gratitude the following consultants and reviewers —our partners in the development of *Workplace Plus*.

## Regional Consultant Board

The following people have participated on an ongoing basis in shaping the content and approach of *Workplace Plus*:

**Ann Belletire**, Northern Illinois University–Business and Industry Services, Oak Brook, Illinois • **Sandra Bergman**, Instructional Facilitator, Alternative, Adult, and Continuing Education Program, New York City Board of Education • **Sherie Burnette**, Assistant Dean, Workforce Education, Brookhaven College of the Dallas County Community College District, Farmers Branch, Texas • **Michael Feher**, Boston Chinatown Neighborhood Center, Boston, Massachusetts • **Susan B. Kanter**, Instructional Supervisor, Continuing Education and Contract Training, Houston Community College-Southwest, Houston, Texas • **Brigitte Marshall**, Consultant, Albany, California • **Monica Oliva**, Educational Specialist, Miami-Dade County Public Schools, Miami, Florida • **Mary E. O'Neill**, Coordinator of Community Education, ESL, Northern Virginia Community College-Annandale Campus, Annandale, Virginia • **Grace Tanaka**, Professor of ESL, Santa Ana College School of Continuing Education; ESL Facilitator, Centennial Education Center, Santa Ana, California • **Marcia L. Taylor**, Workplace Instructor, Joblink, Ispat-Inland Inc., East Chicago, Indiana

## Reviewers

The following people shared their perspectives and made suggestions either by reviewing manuscript or participating in editorial conferences with the authors and editors:

**Leslie Jo Adams**, Santa Ana College–Centennial Education Center, Santa Ana, California • **Sandra Anderson**, El Monte-Rosemead Adult School, El Monte, California • **Marcy Berquist**, San Diego Community College District, San Diego, California • **Ruth Brigham**, A.C.C.E.S.S., Boston, Massachusetts • **Donna Burns**, Mt. San Antonio College, Walnut, California • **Eric Burton**, Downington Area School District, Downington, Pennsylvania • **Michael James Climo**, West Los Angeles College, Culver City, California • **Teresa Costa**, The English Center, Miami, Florida • **Robert Cote**, Miami-Dade County Public Schools, Miami, Florida • **Georgette Davis**, North Orange County Community College District, Orange County, California • **Janet Ennis**, Santa Ana College–Centennial Education Center, Santa Ana, California • **Peggy Fergus**, Northern Illinois University–Business and Industry Services, Oak Brook, Illinois • **Oliva Fernandez**, Hillsborough County Public Schools–Adult & Community Education, Tampa, Florida • **Elizabeth Fitzgerald**, Hialeah Adult & Community Center, Hialeah, Florida • **Marty Furch**, Palomar College, San Diego, California • **Eric Glicker**, North Orange County Community College District, Orange County, California • **Steve Gwynne**, San Diego Community College District, San Diego, California • **Victoria Hathaway**, DePaul University, Chicago, Illinois • **Jeffrey L. Janulis**, Richard J. Daley College, City Colleges of Chicago, Chicago, Illinois • **Mary Karamourtopoulos**, Northern Essex Community College, Haverill, Massachusetts • **Shirley Kelly**, Brookhaven College of the Dallas County Community College District, Farmers Branch, Texas • **Marilou Kessler**, Jewish Vocational Service–Vocational English Program, Chicago, Illinois • **Henry Kim**, North Orange County Community College District, Orange County, California • **Dr. Maria H. Koonce**, Broward County Public Schools, Ft. Lauderdale, Florida • **John Kostovich**, South Texas Community College–Intensive English Program, McAllen, Texas • **Jacques LaCour**, Mt. Diablo Adult Education, Concord, California • **Beatrice Liebman**, Miami Sunset Adult Center, Miami, Florida • **Doris Lorden**, Wright College–Workforce Training Center, Chicago, Illinois • **Mike Lowman**, Coral Gables Adult Education Center, Coral Gables, Florida • **Lois Maharg**, Delaware Technical and Community College • **Vicki Moore**, El Monte-Rosemead Adult School, El Monte, California • **Deborah Nash**, School Board of Palm Beach County Schools, West Palm Beach, Florida • **Cindy Neubrech**, Mt. San Antonio College, Walnut, California • **Patricia Peabody**, Broward County Public Schools, Ft. Lauderdale, Florida • **Joe A. Perez**, Hillsborough County Public Schools, Tampa, Florida • **Diane Pinkley**, Teacher's College, Columbia University, New York, New York • **Kay Powell**, Santa Ana College–Centennial Education Center, Santa Ana, California • **Wendy Rader**, San Diego Community College District, San Diego, California • **Don Robison**, Jewish Vocational Service–Workplace Literacy, Chicago, Illinois • **Richard Sasso**, Triton College, River Grove, Illinois • **Mary Segovia**, El Monte-Rosemead Adult School, El Monte, California • **Laurie Shapero**, Miami-Dade Community College, Miami, Florida • **Sara Shapiro**, El Monte-Rosemead Adult School, El Monte, California • **Samanthia Spence**, Richland College, Dallas, Texas • **JoAnn Stehy**, North Orange County Community College District, Orange County, California • **Margaret Teske**, Mt. San Antonio College, Walnut, California • **Dung Tran**, North Orange County Community College District, Orange County, California • **Claire Valier**, School District of Palm Beach County, West Palm Beach, Florida • **Catherine M. Waterman**, Rancho Santiago Community College, Santa Ana, California • **James Wilson**, Mt. San Antonio College, Walnut, California

# To the teacher

*Workplace Plus: Living and Working in English* is a four-level course in English as a second language. The course prepares adults for self-sufficiency in the three principal areas of their lives: the workplace, the community, and the home. *Workplace Plus* integrates the CASAS life skill competencies and SCANS Competencies and Foundation Skills with a complete language syllabus and relevant social language.

Communicative competence in English is of critical importance in achieving self-sufficiency. *Workplace Plus* applies the best of current second language acquisition research to ensure immediate survival, rapidly enabling learners to
- understand spoken and written general and employment-related language
- communicate in their <u>own</u> words
- understand the culture and behavioral expectations of their new environment and workplace.

In order to achieve these goals with efficiency and speed, *Workplace Plus* weaves together three integrated strands: workplace skills, language, and life skills.

## Course Length
*Workplace Plus* is designed to be used in a period of 60 to 90 classroom hours. This period can be shortened or lengthened, based on the needs of the group or the program. The Teacher's Edition gives detailed instructions for tailoring *Workplace Plus* to specific settings, circumstances, and student groups.

## Components
### Student's Book
The *Workbook Plus* Student's Book is a complete four-skills text, integrating listening, speaking, reading, and writing, with lifeskills, math skills, civics concepts, and authentic practice in understanding native speech and real-life documents. The book contains 10 units, each one culminating in a concise review section.

The Correlations Charts on pages iv–v indicate how *Workplace Plus* is correlated to the following national and state standards:
- SCANS competencies
- CASAS Life Skill Competencies
- EFF Content Standards
- Florida State Standards
- Texas State Standards

These correlations can also be downloaded at no cost from <u>www.longman.com/correlations</u>.

To assist in lesson planning, the Scope and Sequence chart (on pages vi–ix) clearly spells out the following elements for each unit:
- Workplace Skills and Lifeskills
- Grammar
- Grammar Booster
- Social language
- Vocabulary
- Civics/culture concepts
- Math concepts and practical math skills
- Critical thinking skills

In order to facilitate student-centered instruction, *Workplace Plus* uses a variety of grouping strategies: pairs, groups, and whole class. In numerous activities, learners work with others to create a joint product. Those activities are labeled collaborative activities.

Two special features of the *Workplace Plus* Student's Book are <u>Do it yourself!</u> and <u>Authentic practice</u>.

Because learners have an immediate need to use their new language outside the class, <u>Do it yourself!</u> provides a daily opportunity for students of diverse abilities

---

\* *Literacy Plus*, which precedes *Workplace Plus 1*, serves the combined ESL, literacy, and civics needs of the pre-literate beginner.

to put new language into their own words. This affords them a chance to "try their wings" in the safe and supportive environment of the classroom.

Authentic practice activities create a "living language laboratory" within the classroom. Learners practice responding to authentic models of spoken and written English with the language they know. In this way, students build their confidence and skill in coping with the language of the real world.

As a supplement to the Practical grammar section in each *Workplace Plus* unit, the Student's Book includes a comprehensive Grammar Booster at the back of the book. The Grammar Booster provides abundant additional practice for each grammar point taught in the Student's Book units. It also includes grammar charts so that students can review the grammar forms and "Things to remember" before they do an exercise. The Grammar Booster exercises can be done any time after the grammar has been introduced on the Practical grammar pages, either in class or as homework. For your convenience, a separate Answer Key is available.

## Audiocassettes and Audio CDs
Because listening comprehension is a fundamental survival and success skill for new speakers of English, *Workplace Plus* includes a comprehensive listening strand in each unit of the Student's Book. In addition to listening comprehension activities, there are numerous other opportunities for learners to practice their listening skills. All exercises that appear on audio CD or audiocassette are marked with a 🎧 symbol. A transcript of each listening comprehension activity is located on its corresponding Teacher's Edition page, for easy reference.

## Teacher's Edition
An interleaved Teacher's Edition provides reduced Student's Book pages accompanied by page-by-page teaching suggestions that add value to the Student's Book. In addition to general and day-by-day teaching suggestions, each teacher's page includes optional activities, language and culture notes that will help teachers demystify and explain new language to students, answers to all exercises, and the tapescript of each listening comprehension activity.

## Workbook
In addition to the ample opportunities for reading and writing practice contained in the Student's Book, the *Workplace Plus* Workbook contains further reading and writing exercises. The Workbook is valuable for homework or for in-class activities. An added feature is a test preparation activity for each unit, which readies learners for "bubbling in" and coping with the formats of standardized language tests.

## Teacher's Resource Binder
A three-ring binder contains a wealth of valuable items to enable busy teachers to customize their instruction and make the preparation of supplementary teaching aids unnecessary. The Classroom Booster Pack provided with the Binder features pair-work cards, vocabulary flash cards, grammar self-checks, photo chat cards, and extension activities for daily use. Correlations of *Workplace Plus* with state and federal standards are also included in the Binder.

The following additional teacher-support materials are also available: Student Progress Checklists, Pre- and Post-Tests and Achievement Tests, Skills for Test Taking, and industry-specific Job Packs that are correlated with Student's Books 1 and 2.

## Do it yourself! Transparencies
A special feature of the *Workplace Plus* series is the full-page Do it Yourself! illustration located at the end of each unit. This open-ended activity is designed to elicit from students all the language they know— vocabulary, social language, and grammar. The picture provides a clear visual context for practice and helps students bridge the

gap between language practice and authentic language use. The full-page illustrations are available as four-color transparencies to be used with an overhead projector. The <u>Do it yourself!</u> transparencies come in a convenient, resealable envelope, along with a Teacher's Notes booklet containing suggested activities.

<u>Placement Test</u>
A simple-to-administer test places students accurately within the *Workplace Plus* series.

<u>*Workplace Plus* Companion Website</u>
The *Workplace Plus* companion website (www.longman.com/workplaceplus) provides numerous additional resources for students and teachers. This no-cost, high-benefit feature includes opportunities for further practice of language and content from the *Workplace Plus* Student's Book. For the teacher, there are optional strategies and materials that amplify the *Workplace Plus* Teacher's Edition.

**Student's Book unit contents**
Each unit in the *Workplace Plus* Student's Book uses an integrated five-step approach.

1. <u>Vocabulary</u>
   Essential vocabulary is presented in a picture dictionary format and followed by exercises.

2. <u>Practical conversations</u>
   Simple, memorable model conversations that are transferable to learners' own lives permit intensive practice of vocabulary and key social language. These are followed by lively pair-work activities.

3. <u>Practical grammar</u>
   Essential grammatical structure practice enables learners to manipulate the vocabulary and practical conversations to express ideas of their own.

4. <u>Authentic practice 1</u>
   A unique, real-world listening and speaking rehearsal, in which learners build their confidence and ability to interact in the world beyond the classroom.

5. <u>Authentic practice 2</u>
   A unique, real-world reading and writing rehearsal, in which learners build their confidence and skill to understand and use authentic documents that they will encounter in their own lives.

<u>Review</u>
Following each unit is a two-page review for learners to check their progress.

## Authors

### Joan Saslow

Joan Saslow has taught English as a second language and English as a foreign language to adults and young adults in the United States and Chile. She taught workplace English at the General Motors auto assembly plant in Tarrytown, NY; and Adult ESL at Westchester Community College and at Marymount College in New York. In addition, Ms. Saslow taught English and French at the Binational Centers of Valparaíso and Viña del Mar, Chile, and the Catholic University of Valparaíso.

Ms. Saslow is the series director of Longman's popular five-level adult series *True Colors, an EFL Course for Real Communication* and of *True Voices*, a five-level video course. She is the author of *English in Context: Reading Comprehension for Science and Technology*, a three-level series for English for special purposes. In addition, Ms. Saslow has been an editor of language teaching materials, a teacher trainer, and a frequent speaker at gatherings of ESL and EFL teachers for over thirty years.

### Tim Collins

Tim Collins has taught English as a second language and English as a foreign language to adults and young adults in the United States, Spain, and Morocco. He taught English for special purposes at the Intensive English Institute of the University of Illinois at Urbana. Dr. Collins also taught high school ESL at Lycée Al Badissi, Al Hoceima, Morocco, and advanced English composition at the University of Barcelona. In addition, he taught college Spanish at the University of Illinois at Urbana.

Dr. Collins is Assistant Professor of Language Minority Education at National-Louis University in Chicago, where he teaches in a teacher training program. In addition, he has been a writer and editor of English as a second language and adult education materials for over twelve years. He is a frequent speaker at professional ESL meetings. Dr. Collins's Ph.D. degree is from the University of Texas at Austin.

## Series advisor

### Edwina Hoffman

Edwina Hoffman has taught English for speakers of other languages in South Florida and at the Miccosukee Tribe of Indians, and English as a foreign language in Venezuela. She provided teacher training in a seven-state area for federally funded multi-functional resource centers serving the southeastern part of the United States. Dr. Hoffman taught English composition at Florida International University and graduate ESOL methods at the University of Miami.

Dr. Hoffman is an instructional supervisor with the adult and vocational programs of Miami-Dade County Public Schools in Miami, Florida. She has acted as a consultant, reviewer, and author of adult ESOL materials for over twenty years. A graduate of Middlebury College, Dr. Hoffman's doctoral degree is from Florida International University.

# Welcome to *Workplace Plus*

 **Vocabulary**

## Classroom actions

🎧 **A.** Look at the pictures. Listen.

listen

read

talk

repeat

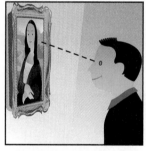

look

point

circle

write

🎧 **B.** Listen again and repeat.

🎧 **C.** Now listen and point to the pictures.

## D. Look and write.

| write | read | listen | point |
|---|---|---|---|

1. _read_

2. _____

3. _____

4. _____

 **Practical conversations**

---

**Conversation 1  Greetings and introductions**

🎧 **A. Listen and read.**

Hello. I'm Carmen.

Hi, Carmen. I'm Mark.

Nice to meet you, Mark.

Nice to meet you too.

**∩ B. Listen again and repeat.**

**C.** Pair work.

> **A:** Hello. I'm _____.
> **B:** Hi, _____. I'm _____.
> **A:** Nice to meet you, _____.
> **B:** Nice to meet you too.

---

**Conversation 2    More greetings and introductions**

**∩ A. Listen and read.**

> Mark, this is Bruno. Bruno, this is Mark.

> Hi, Mark. Nice to meet you.

> Nice to meet you too.

**∩ B. Listen again and repeat.**

**C.** Group work.

> **A:** _____, this is _____.
> _____, this is _____.
> **B:** Hi, _____. Nice to meet you.
> **C:** Nice to meet you too.

# ➤ Vocabulary

## Classroom words

🎧 **A.** Look at the pictures. Listen.

a number

a letter

Read a book.

a word

Read a book.

a sentence

🎧 **B.** Listen again and repeat.

**C.** Read and write.

1. Write a number. _____

2. Write a letter. _____

3. Circle the word:     s     12     and

## More classroom words

🎧 **A.** Look at the pictures. Listen.

a picture

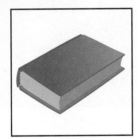

a book

a teacher     a class

a partner    a partner

classmates

🎧 **B.** Listen again and repeat.

**C.** Look and point.

1. Point to a book.
2. Point to a picture in the classroom.

## Names and addresses

🎧 **A.** Look and listen.

a name

Jeffrey Chang

an address

76 King Street, Watertown, CT   06795

a zip code

(203) 555-3222

a phone number

🎧 **B.** Listen again and repeat.

**C.** Read and write.

1. Write your name. _____

2. Write your address. _____

3. Write your zip code. _____

## The alphabet

🎧 **A.** Listen and read.

| Aa | Bb | Cc | Dd | Ee | Ff | Gg | Hh | Ii |
|----|----|----|----|----|----|----|----|----|
| Jj | Kk | Ll | Mm | Nn | Oo | Pp | Qq | Rr |
| Ss | Tt | Uu | Vv | Ww | Xx | Yy | Zz | |

🎧 **B.** Listen again and repeat.

## Conversations 1 and 2    Spelling names

🎧 **A.** **Listen and read.**

🎧 **B.** **Listen again and repeat.**

**C.** Pair work. **Ask about spelling a name.**

**A:** Hi, I'm _____.

**B:** _____. Is that _____?

**A:** _____.

**A. Listen and read.**

**B. Listen again and repeat.**

    **A:** What's your name, please?

    **B:** _____.

    **A:** Is that your first name?

    **B:** Yes, it is.

    **A:** And what's your last name?

    **B:** My last name is _____.

    **A:** Thank you, _____.

# ➤ Vocabulary

## Numbers 0–10

 **A. Listen and read.**

| 0 | zero | 4 | four | 8 | eight |
|---|------|---|------|---|-------|
| 1 | one | 5 | five | 9 | nine |
| 2 | two | 6 | six | 10 | ten |
| 3 | three | 7 | seven | | |

 **B. Listen again and repeat.**

# ➤ Practical conversation

## Conversation   Addresses

 **A. Listen and read.**

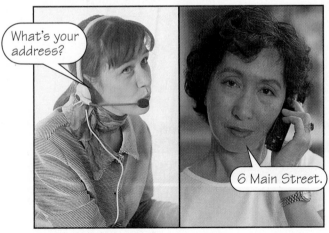

What's your address?

6 Main Street.

Thanks.

You're welcome.

 **B. Listen again and repeat.**

# Vocabulary

## Numbers 11–100

 **A.** Listen and read.

| | | | | | |
|---|---|---|---|---|---|
| 11 | eleven | 21 | twenty-one | 31 | thirty-one |
| 12 | twelve | 22 | twenty-two | 40 | forty |
| 13 | thirteen | 23 | twenty-three | 50 | fifty |
| 14 | fourteen | 24 | twenty-four | 60 | sixty |
| 15 | fifteen | 25 | twenty-five | 70 | seventy |
| 16 | sixteen | 26 | twenty-six | 80 | eighty |
| 17 | seventeen | 27 | twenty-seven | 90 | ninety |
| 18 | eighteen | 28 | twenty-eight | 100 | one hundred |
| 19 | nineteen | 29 | twenty-nine | | |
| 20 | twenty | 30 | thirty | | |

**B.** Listen again and repeat.

# Practical conversations

## Conversation 1    More addresses

**A.** Listen and read.

🎧 **B.** Listen again and repeat.

**C.** Pair work. **Ask your partner for an address.**

> **A:** What's your address?
> **B:** _____.
> **A:** _____.
> **B:** You're welcome.

---

## Conversation 2  Telephone numbers and area codes

🎧 **A.** Listen and read.

🎧 **B.** Listen again and repeat.

**C.** Pair work. **Ask your partner for a telephone number.**

> **A:** What's your phone number?
> **B:** _____.
> **A:** And your area code?
> **B:** _____.

**Create conversations. Use your <u>own</u> words.**

Introduce two classmates.

Ask about first name and last name.

Ask about spelling a name.

Ask for an address.

Ask for a telephone number.

# Your life and work

 **Vocabulary**

## Picture dictionary

🎧 **A.** Listen.

### Occupations

1. a plumber
2. a homemaker
3. a cook
4. a cashier
5. a manager
6. a housekeeper
7. a teacher
8. a student
9. a bus driver
10. a mechanic
11. an engineer
12. an electrician

🎧 **B.** Listen again and repeat.

🎧 **C.** Now listen and point to the pictures.

🎧 **How to say it**

a teacher          an electrician

**D.** Write the occupations. Use the words from the box.

| | | | |
|---|---|---|---|
| a cashier | a plumber | a teacher | a manager |
| a bus driver | a cook | ~~an engineer~~ | a mechanic |

1. _an engineer_

2. _____

3. _____

4. _____

5. _____

6. _____

7. _____

8. _____

## ➤ Do it yourself!

**Write.**

Your occupation: _____

## Practical conversations

### Models 1 and 2   Meet and greet other students.

🎧 **A.** Listen and read.

A: Are you Ken Wang?
B: Yes, I am.
A: Oh, hi, Ken. Nice to meet you.
   I'm Luis Lopez.

A: Are you Ana?
C: No, I'm not. I'm Marie. Marie Laporte.
A: Oh, hi, Marie. Good to meet you.
   I'm Luis Lopez.

🎧 **B.** Listen again and repeat.

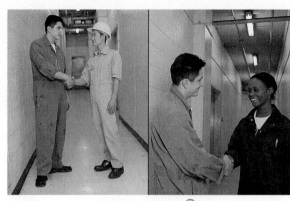

🎧 **Greetings**
Nice to meet you.
Good to meet you.

**C.** Pair work. **Now use your own names.**

A: Are you _____?
B: _____.
A: Oh, hi, _____. Good to meet you. I'm _____.

### Model 3   Where are you from?

🎧 **A.** Listen and read.

A: Where are you from?
B: China. What about you?
A: I'm from Mexico.

🎧 **B.** Listen again and repeat.

**C.** Pair work. **Now talk about your own countries.**

A: Where are you from?
B: _____. What about you?
A: I'm from _____.

**A. Listen and read.**

A: What do you do?

B: I'm a mechanic. And you?

A: I'm a cashier. But right now I'm unemployed.

B: Oh, I'm sorry. Well, good luck!

A: Thanks!

**B. Listen again and repeat.**

**C. Pair work. Now use your <u>own</u> occupations.**

A: What do you do?

B: I'm _____. And you?

A: I'm _____.

# ➤ Do it yourself!

**Complete the chart. Talk to two students. Ask:**

- What's your name?
- Where are you from?
- What do you do?

I'm Maria.
I'm from Mexico.
I'm a bus driver.

| Name | From | Occupation |
|------|------|------------|
| Maria | Mexico | bus driver |
| **1.** | | |
| **2.** | | |

## The verb be

| | | | | |
|---|---|---|---|---|
| I **am** | | | | |
| You **are** | | | | |
| He **is** | a cook. | | | |
| She **is** | | | | |
| Marta **is** | | | | |

| | | | |
|---|---|---|---|
| I **am** | | | |
| You **are** | | | |
| He **is** | **not** a teacher. | | |
| She **is** | | | |
| Marta **is** | | | |

🎧 **Contractions**

| I + am | = I'm |
|---|---|
| you + are | = you're |
| he + is | = he's |
| she + is | = she's |
| Marta + is | = Marta's |

**A.** Complete the sentences. Write <u>am</u>, <u>are</u>, or <u>is</u>.

1. Yuri ___is___ from Russia.

2. You _____ a student.

3. He _____ unemployed.

4. I _____ not an engineer.

5. She _____ not from Greece.

6. Blanca _____ my partner.

**B.** Write about the pictures. Write <u>He's</u> or <u>She's</u>. Write <u>a</u> or <u>an</u>.

1. *She's an engineer.* _____

2. *He's a cashier.* _____

3. _____

4. _____

| Is she<br>Is he | a teacher? | Yes, she is. / No, she's not.<br>Yes, he is. / No, he's not. |

🎧 **Contractions**

| I am + not | = | I'm not |
| you are + not | = | you're not |
| he is + not | = | he's not |
| she is + not | = | she's not |
| Marta is + not | = | Marta's not |

**C.** **Complete each conversation. Circle the letter.**

1. **A:** Are you a cashier?
   **B:** _____
   **a.** No, I'm not.   **b.** Yes, he is.

2. **A:** Is Rosa from California?
   **B:** _____
   **a.** Rosa.   **b.** Yes, she is.

3. **A:** _____
   **B:** No, she's not.
   **a.** Is he a plumber?   **b.** Is she a plumber?

4. **A:** _____
   **B:** Yes, I am.
   **a.** Are you a student?   **b.** Is he a student?

➤ Do it yourself!

**A.** **Pair work.** **Point. Talk about the people.**
**Ask and answer questions.**

A: *Is he an electrician?*
B: *No, he's a manager.*

**B.** **Personalization.** **Now tell your partner**
**about yourself.**

*I'm a homemaker.*

**With words you know, YOU can talk to this clerk.**

## A. Listen and read.

**Clerk:** May I help you, please?

**YOU** *Yes, thank you. I'm Kathy Carter.*

**Clerk:** Is that Kathy with a C or with a K?

**YOU** *A K.*

**Clerk:** And what's your occupation, Ms. Carter?

**YOU** *I'm a cashier right now.*

**Clerk:** And are you from Parkville?

**YOU** *Yes, I am.*

**Clerk:** OK, good. Please fill out this form.

## B. Listen to the clerk. Read your part.

## C. Listen and read. Choose your response. Circle the letter.

1. "May I help you, please?"

   **a.** You're welcome.          **b.** Yes, thanks.

2. "Is that with an R?"

   **a.** Yes.                     **b.** Thank you.

3. "What's your occupation?"

   **a.** I'm a mechanic.          **b.** I'm from China.

## D. Listen. Choose your response. Circle the letter.

1. **a.** I'm from Mexico.         **b.** Well, good luck.

2. **a.** Kathy Carter.            **b.** I'm a cashier.

3. **a.** No, I'm not.             **b.** Yes, thank you.

🎧 **A.** Look at the forms. Listen to the conversations.

1.

🚂 **CENTRAL HOTEL**

● Employment Application

NAME: ___Dumont___  ___Cara___   OCCUPATION: _____
      Last Name    First Name

2.

**AC E COMPANY**

**Employment Application**                                    Date: **11/13/02**

NAME: ___Lobo___  ___Carlos___   OCCUPATION: _____
      Last Name   First Name

ADDRESS: ___521 Green St.___   ___San Francisco___   ___CA___   ___94114___
         Number and Street          City              State      ZIP Code

3.

🌿 Garden Street Adult School                              DATE: _2/24/01_

NAME: _____Ivan_____
         Last Name              First Name

ADDRESS: __76 Low Street__   __Seattle__            __WA__   __98109__
         Number and Street      City                State     ZIP Code

TELEPHONE: (_205_) __555-2156__          NATIONALITY: ___Russian___

OCCUPATION: ___Taxi driver___            COURSE: _Beginning English_

🎧 **B.** Now listen again and complete the forms.

## ➤ Do it yourself!

**A.** Write your <u>own</u> response. Then read your conversation out loud with a partner.

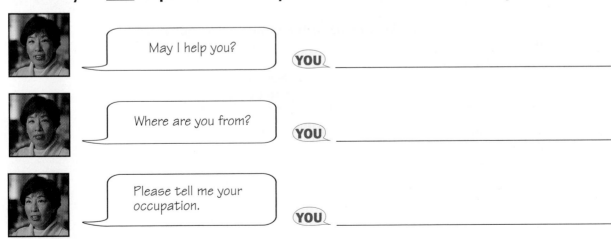

May I help you?        **YOU** _____

Where are you from?    **YOU** _____

Please tell me your occupation.   **YOU** _____

**B.** Discussion. Talk about another student or about a person at work.

## Authentic practice 2

### Reading

**A.** Look at the list of workers.

**Current Employees**

| | | | | |
|---|---|---|---|---|
| Cruz, Pilar | **driver** | | Rahman, Lisa | **cook** |
| Hong, Peggy | **cook** | | Solano, Cristina | **housekeeper** |
| Lee, Min | **housekeeper** | | Thomas, David | **driver** |
| Mendoza, Ines | **housekeeper** | | Vargas, Juan | **housekeeper** |
| Metz, Paul | **cook** | | Yu, Bryan | **manager** |

**B.** Check ☑ <u>yes</u> or <u>no</u>.

| | yes | no |
|---|---|---|
| 1. The list is from the Bedford Hospital. | ❑ | ❑ |
| 2. The list is from the Bedford Hotel. | ❑ | ❑ |

**C.** Critical thinking. **Read the list.
Write the number of people.**

1. ___3___ cooks

2. _____ housekeepers

3. _____ drivers

4. _____ manager

🎧 **How to say it**

**a** student      student**s**

**D.** Collaborative activity. **Make a chart of the students in <u>your</u> class.
Write the occupations. Write the number of students.**

| Occupations | Number of students |
|---|---|
| _taxi drivers_ | _2_ |
| | |
| | |

20     Unit 1

# ➤ Do it yourself!

**1.** Point. Say the occupations.

*A bus driver*

**2.** Point. Ask questions.

*Is he a student?*

**3.** Create conversations for the people.

*A: What do you do?*
*B: I'm a cashier.*

**4.** Say more about the picture. Use your <u>own</u> words. Say as much as you can.

Now I can talk about
❑ names.
❑ occupations.
❑ where I am from.
❑ _____.

# Your environment

## Vocabulary

**Objectives**
- talk about places
- ask for directions
- give directions

### Picture dictionary

①
② 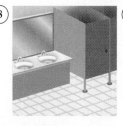 U.S. Post Office
③
④  NATIONAL ADULT SCHOOL
⑤  RESTAURANT

⑥
⑦
⑧
⑨
⑩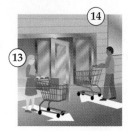

⑪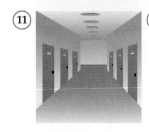
⑫
⑬ ⑭
⑮ ⑯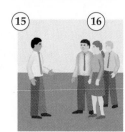
⑰ ⑱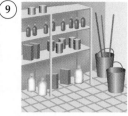

🎧 **A.** Listen.

| Workplaces | | Rooms and other places | | Other words |
|---|---|---|---|---|
| ① a hospital | ⑤ a restaurant | ⑧ a restroom | ⑫ an office | ⑮ a person |
| ② a post office | ⑥ a supermarket | ⑨ a supply room | ⑬ an exit | ⑯ people |
| ③ a bank | ⑦ a parking lot | ⑩ a meeting room | ⑭ an entrance | ⑰ old |
| ④ a school | | ⑪ a hall | | ⑱ new |

🎧 **B.** Listen again and repeat.

🎧 **C.** Now listen and point to the pictures.

at home

at work

at school

at 22 Church Street

🎧 **How to say it**

in the restroom
in the parking lot
in the supply room
in the meeting room

**D.** Write the name of each place. Write **a** or **an**.

1. *a meeting room*

2. _____

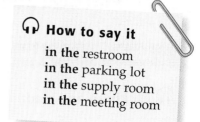

3. _____

4. _____

5. _____

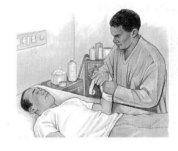

6. _____

## ➤ Do it yourself!

**A.** Write the names of other rooms or places. Write **a** or **an**.

1. _*a kitchen*_
2. _____
3. _____
4. _____

**B.** **Pair work.** Read your words to your partner.

## Practical conversations

### Model 1   Ask about people.

🎧 **A. Listen and read.**

> **A:** Are Sandra and Elena here?
> **B:** No, they're not. They're in the office.
> **A:** Excuse me?
> **B:** They're in the office.

🎧 **B. Listen again and repeat.**

**C. Pair work. Now ask about real people.**

> **A:** Are _____ and _____ here?
> **B:** No, they're not. They're _____.
> **A:** Excuse me?
> **B:** They're _____.

### Model 2   Ask about places.

🎧 **A. Listen and read.**

> **A:** Where are the restrooms?
> **B:** They're down the hall, on the right.

🎧 **B. Listen again and repeat.**

**C. Pair work. Now ask about places on the map.**

> **A:** Where are the _____s?
> **B:** They're down the hall, on _____.

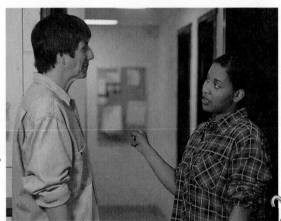

| Office | Office | Supply room 1 | Supply room 2 |
|---|---|---|---|

Hall

| Meeting room | Meeting room | Restroom | Restroom |
|---|---|---|---|

**Left and Right**

Left                                    Right
←                                          →

## A. Listen and read.

**A:** Excuse me. I'm looking for the post office.

**B:** The post office? It's on Main Street. It's next to the bank.

**A:** Thanks.

**B:** You're welcome.

## B. Listen again and repeat.

## C. Pair work. Now talk about places on the map.

**A:** Excuse me. I'm looking for the _____.

**B:** The _____? It's _____.

**A:** _____.

**B:** You're welcome.

### How to say it

It's **on** Main Street.

It's **across from** the bank.

It's **between** the bank **and** the school.

It's **next to** the bank.

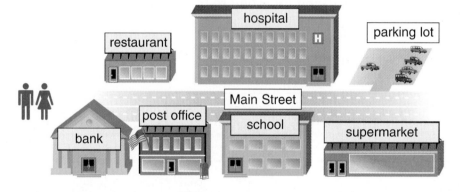

## ▶ Do it yourself!

**Pair work. Create a conversation from the picture. Ask for directions. Give directions.**

**Practical grammar**

## Be: plural

| We | | | We | | |
|---|---|---|---|---|---|
| You | } | **are** in the supply room. | You | } | **are not** in the office. |
| They | | | They | | |

🎧 **Contractions**

we
you } + are = we're / you're / they're
they

we are + not = we're not

**A.** Complete the conversations. Write <u>We're</u>, <u>You're</u>, <u>They're</u>, or <u>they're</u>.

1. **A:** Are Sandra and Elena here?

   **B:** No, they're not. _____ in the office.

2. **A:** Are we in Meeting Room A?

   **B:** No, we're not. _____ in Meeting Room B.

3. **A:** Where are they? In the parking lot?

   **B:** No, _____ not in the parking lot. They're in the supply room.

4. **A:** Are the offices down the hall?

   **B:** No, _____ across from the meeting room.

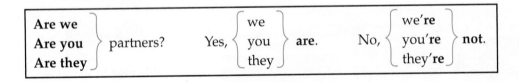

| Are we | | | | we | | | | we're | |
|---|---|---|---|---|---|---|---|---|---|
| Are you | } | partners? | Yes, | you | } | are. | No, | you're | } not. |
| Are they | | | | they | | | | they're | |

**B.** Complete the conversations. Write the words on the line.

1. **A:** Are they in the supply room?

   **B:** No, _____ not.

2. **A:** Allen and Eva, _____ engineers?

   **B:** Yes, we are.

3. **A:** _____ here?

   **B:** Yes, but they're in the restroom right now.

| | |
|---|---|
| **Where**'s the post office? | It's on Main Street. |
| **What**'s your occupation? | I'm a cashier in the new restaurant. |
| **Who** are they? | Mary and Carmen. |

**C.** Complete the questions. Choose words. Write the words on the line.

1. _Where_ are Luis and Paco?    In the parking lot.
   What / Where

2. _____ your address?    It's 10 Main Street.
   What's / Who's

3. Excuse me. _____ the bank?    It's on Water Street.
   Who's / Where's

4. _____ in the parking lot?    Donna.
   Who's / What's

5. _____ are you from?    Guatemala.
   What / Where

## ➤ Do it yourself!

**A.** Ask questions about the picture.
**Use Where, Who, and What.**

A: *Where's the restaurant?*
B: *It's next to the school.*

**B.** Personalization. **Now tell your partner about a place in your neighborhood.**

*The bank is between the supermarket and the parking lot.*

## Authentic practice 1

🎧 **A.** Listen and read.

**Man:** May I help you?

**YOU** *Yes. I'm looking for Manuel's Restaurant.*

**Man:** Manuel's? It's right around the corner. On Hill Street. Do you know where that is?

**YOU** *Hill Street? Yes.*

**Man:** Well, Manuel's is down that street . . . in the new building next to the parking lot. It's on the right-hand side of the street.

**YOU** *Excuse me?*

**Man:** It's on Hill Street. On the right. Next to the parking lot.

**YOU** *Thanks.*

**Man:** Sure. No problem.

🎧 **B.** Listen to the man. Read <u>your</u> part.

🎧 **C.** Listen and read. Choose <u>your</u> response. Circle the letter.

1. "Do you know where the parking lot is?"

   **a.** Oh, yes. It's next to Green's Supermarket.  **b.** Thanks.

2. "It's on the right side of the street."

   **a.** Well, good luck!  **b.** Next to the post office?

3. "It's right around the corner."

   **a.** I'm looking for the school.  **b.** On Lake Street?

🎧 **D.** Listen. Choose <u>your</u> response. Circle the letter.

1. **a.** Thank you very much.  **b.** Excuse me?

2. **a.** Next to the parking lot? Good.  **b.** Oh, yes.

3. **a.** Yes. I'm looking for the bank.  **b.** Yes. Excuse me.

Listen to the conversations. Then listen again. Write the place on the map.

1. Where's the supply room?

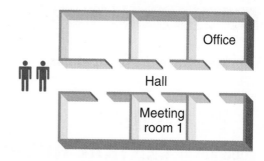

2. Where's the supermarket?

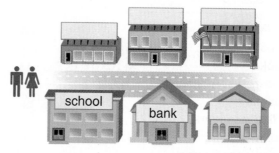

3. Where's the hospital?

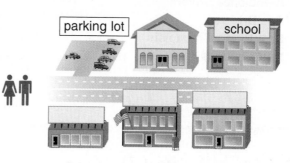

## ➤ Do it yourself!

**A.** Use the map from question 3. Write your <u>own</u> response. Then read your conversation out loud with a partner.

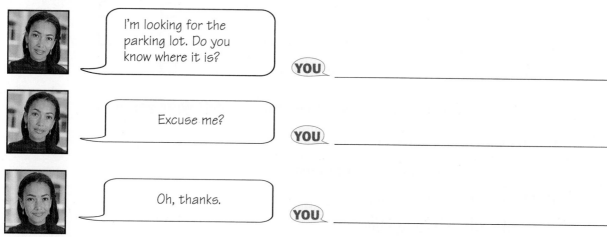

I'm looking for the parking lot. Do you know where it is?

YOU _____

Excuse me?

YOU _____

Oh, thanks.

YOU _____

**B.** Discussion. Talk about places at work or in the neighborhood.

## Reading

**A.** Look at the poster. Circle the occupations.

> ## HELP WANTED
> Get a good job at **CENTRAL HOSPITAL!**
>
> **NOW HIRING:**
>
> Housekeepers
> Cooks
> Pharmacist Assistants
> Cashiers
> Office Managers
> Plumbers
> Ambulance Drivers
> Bus Drivers
> Respiratory Therapists
> Nurse's Aides
>
> **Open interviews
> Saturday, November 12
> 9 a.m. to 5 p.m.**
>
> Central Hospital
> 1200 West Street
> Dallas, Texas  79702
> (217) 555-7524
>
> The hospital is across from the Bank of Texas.
> Park in the lot next to the bank.

**B.** Now read the poster. Check ☑ yes or no.

|  | yes | no |
|---|---|---|
| 1. The name of the workplace is Central Hospital. | ☐ | ☐ |
| 2. It's on Dallas Street. | ☐ | ☐ |
| 3. The zip code is 75240. | ☐ | ☐ |
| 4. Central Hospital is looking for office managers. | ☐ | ☐ |
| 5. The hospital is next to the Bank of Texas. | ☐ | ☐ |

**C.** Critical thinking. **Can they get jobs at Central Hospital? Write yes or no.**

1. Mia Kim is a bus driver.  _yes_

2. Todd Williams is a restaurant manager.  _____

3. Hillary Dennis is a cook.  _____

4. Sandra Morin is a teacher.  _____

5. Kevin Chung is a mechanic.  _____

**A.** Make a map of a workplace. Write the rooms and other places on your map.
Use words from the box.

| supply room | restrooms | entrance | office | meeting room |

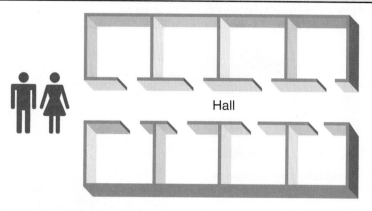

Hall

**B.** Complete these notes about your map.

*I'm in the office right now. It's*

_____

_____ .

Hi:
The books are in the supply room.
The supply room is _____

_____ .

**C.** Discussion. Compare your map and notes with your partner's map and notes.

## ➤ Do it yourself!    A class project

**A.** Collaborative activity.
Write a list of places in the
neighborhood. Then make a
map on the chalkboard.

**B.** Discussion.
Talk about the map.

**A.** Vocabulary. **Look at the pictures. Write places from the box. Write <u>a</u> or <u>an</u>.**

| post office | supply room | office | parking lot |

1. _____

2. _____

3. _____

4. _____

**B.** Vocabulary. **Complete the sentences.**

1. The bank is _____ the post office.

2. The hospital is _____ the parking lot.

**C.** Conversation. **Choose <u>your</u> response. Circle the letter.**

1. "Are Petra and Evan here?"

   **a.** No, they're at work.          **b.** They're Petra and Evan.

2. "Excuse me. I'm looking for the old school."

   **a.** Where is the school?          **b.** It's across from the parking lot.

3. "Thanks."

   **a.** No problem.          **b.** It's down the hall.

**D.** Grammar. **Complete the sentences. Write <u>is</u>, <u>Are</u>, or <u>'re not</u>.**

1. **A:** Where _____ the hospital?

   **B:** The hospital _____ next to the bank.

2. **A:** _____ you in Meeting Room 1?

   **B:** No, we_____.

**E.** Writing. **Answer the questions.**

1. Where is the supermarket?    _On Main Street. Next to the bank._

2. Where is <u>your</u> supermarket? _____

3. Where is <u>your</u> school?    _____

➤ Do it yourself!

1. Point. Name the places.
   *A bank*

2. Point. Talk about the people.
   *They're students.*

3. Create conversations for the people.
   *A: Excuse me. Where's the post office?*
   *B: It's across from the restaurant.*

4. Say more about the picture. Use your <u>own</u> words. Say as much as you can.

Now I can
❑ talk about places.
❑ ask for directions.
❑ give directions.
❑ _____.

# Your equipment and machines

## Vocabulary

### Picture dictionary

Directions
Close the lid.
Press START.

beep
beep
beep

## 🎧 A. Listen.

| Machines | | Parts of machines | Actions | |
|---|---|---|---|---|
| ① a copier | ⑤ a coffee maker | ⑧ a button | ⑬ open | ⑰ unplug |
| ② a computer | ⑥ a lawn mower | ⑨ a key | ⑭ close | ⑱ call |
| ③ a telephone | ⑦ a cash register | ⑩ a door | ⑮ press | |
| ④ a microwave | | ⑪ a lid | ⑯ turn | |
| | | ⑫ directions | | |

## 🎧 B. Listen again and repeat.

## 🎧 C. Now listen and point to the pictures.

🎧 **How to say it**

off          on

**D.** Match the pictures and the sentences. Write the letter on the line.

1. ___e___

2. _____

3. _____

4. _____

5. _____

a. Read the directions.

b. Call Mr. Ruvo, please.
   His number is 555–2144.

c. Turn the key.

d. Press the button.

e. Unplug the machine, please.

## ➤ Do it yourself!

**A.** Collaborative activity. Complete the chart. Use machines from page 36. Or use your **own** machines. Write **a** or **an**.

| a button | a key | a lid or door |
|---|---|---|
| a copier | | |
| | | |
| | | |

**B.** Read your chart to your class.

## Model 1   Make a suggestion. Get help.

**A. Listen and read.**

> A: Oh, no!
> B: What's wrong?
> A: The cash register is out of order.
> B: Let's call Ms. Rivas.
> A: Good idea.

**B. Listen again and repeat.**

**C. Pair work. Now use your <u>own</u> words.**

> A: Oh, no!
> B: What's wrong?
> A: The _____ is out of order.
> B: Let's call _____.
> A: Good idea.

## Models 2 and 3   Give directions. Give a warning.

**A. Listen and read.**

> A: Press the <u>on</u> button.
> B: OK.
>
> A: Don't press the <u>off</u> button.
> B: No problem.

**B. Listen again and repeat.**

**How to say it**

Don't open the door!

**C. Pair work. Now use the pictures. Or talk about your <u>own</u> machine.**

> A: _____ the _____.
> B: _____.

**A.** Listen and read.

    **A:** How do I start the coffee maker?
    **B:** Press the <u>on</u> button.
    **A:** OK. And how do I start the microwave?
    **B:** I don't know.

**B.** Listen again and repeat.

**C.** Pair work. **Now use the pictures or your <u>own</u> machines.**

    **A:** How do I start the _____?
    **B:** _____.
    **A:** OK. And how do I start the _____?
    **B:** I don't know.

# ➤ Do it yourself!

Pair work. **Create a conversation for the people about machines. Use your <u>own</u> words.**

### Suggestions with Let's

**A.** Complete the suggestions. Use **Let's**.

1. **A:** Oh, no!

   **B:** What's wrong?

   **A:** The new cash register's out of order.

   **B:** _____ John.

   **A:** OK. What's the number?

2. **A:** _____ the computer.

   **B:** OK. Press the <u>on</u> button.

3. **A:** How do I start the copier?

   **B:** I don't know. _____ the directions.

   **A:** Good idea.

**B.** Write suggestions with **Let's**. Use the words in the box.

| call the manager | close the door | ~~start the computer~~ | open the door |
|---|---|---|---|

1. _Let's start the computer._ _____

2. _____

3. _____

4. _____

> **Press** the <u>on</u> button.     **Turn** the key, please.

**C.** **Complete the sentences. Write the words from the box.**

> | Call | open | ~~Press~~ | Turn |
> |---|---|---|---|

1. Start the coffee maker. _Press_ the <u>on</u> button.

2. Let's start the lawn mower. _____ the key.

3. _____ the manager. The phone number is 555–4801.

4. Please _____ the lid of the copier.

> **Negative commands**
> **Don't press** the <u>off</u> button.     **Don't unplug** the computer, please.

**D.** **Write negative commands. Choose a verb. Use <u>Don't</u>.**

1. _Don't start_ the lawn mower.
   start / open

2. _____ the copier, please.
   call / unplug

3. Please _____ the coffee maker.
   start / close

4. _____ the <u>on</u> button.
   start / press

5. _____ the door of the microwave.
   open / start

➤ **Do it yourself!**

**Give directions to the office workers.**

*Unplug the coffee maker.*

# Authentic practice 1

**With words you know, YOU can talk to this co-worker.**

🎧 **A. Listen and read.**

**Co-worker:** Oh, no. What's the problem?

**YOU** *The machine is out of order.*

**Co-worker:** Again? What's wrong with it?

**YOU** *I don't know.*

**Co-worker:** Well, maybe we need to call the manager.

**YOU** *OK. Good idea. What's the number?*

**Co-worker:** It's extension 3023, I think.

**YOU** *Thanks.*

🎧 **B. Listen to the co-worker. Read your part.**

🎧 **C. Listen and read. Choose your response. Circle the letter.**

1. "What's wrong?"
   **a.** The cash register is out of order.  **b.** It's OK.

2. "Did you turn the key?"
   **a.** Good luck.  **b.** Yes.

3. "Maybe we need to call the manager."
   **a.** OK. What's the number?  **b.** No, it's not.

🎧 **D. Listen. Choose your response. Circle the letter.**

1. **a.** Good idea.  **b.** It's out of order.
2. **a.** 575–1222.  **b.** Mr. Harris.
3. **a.** Oh, yes.  **b.** What's wrong?

**A.** Listen to the conversations. Then read the sentences. Write <u>yes</u> or <u>no</u>.

1. The conversations are about directions for machines. _____

2. The machines are out of order. _____

**B.** Listen again. Read the directions for each machine. Circle the letter.

1.

    **a.** Press <u>on</u>.

    **b.** Press the <u>off</u> button.

2.

    **a.** Turn the key to the right.

    **b.** Turn the key to the left.

3.

    **a.** Close the door and press <u>start</u>.

    **b.** Unplug the microwave.

## ➤ Do it yourself!

**A.** Write your <u>own</u> response. Then read your conversation out loud with a partner.

What's the problem with the machine?

YOU _____

Is it on or off?

YOU _____

Well, if it's really out of order, let's call the manager.

YOU _____

**B.** Discussion. Talk about machines at home or at work.

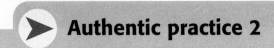
### Reading

**A.** Look at the card. Then write <u>yes</u> or <u>no</u>.

**WORLDWIDE**
TELEPHONE COMPANY

**INSTRUCTIONS**

1. Call 1-800-555-0237.
2. Press the card number. ▶ | 182-508-0510 | Card number
3. Press 1, the area code, and the number you want to call. (For international calls, press 011, the country code, and the number.)

Prepaid Phone Card
**30 minutes**

1. The card is for telephone calls.

_____

2. The card gives directions.

_____

**B.** Critical thinking. **Read the Worldwide Telephone Company card. Then write the directions to call the Good Morning Restaurant.**

1. Call _____.

2. Then press _____.

3. Then press _____.

**Look at the pictures and the directions. Complete the directions.
Write words from the box.**

| card | directions | Press | Press | put | ~~telephone~~ |
|------|-----------|-------|-------|-----|-----------|

**INSTRUCTIONS**

Put 25 cents in the _telephone_ . _____ the
　　　　　　　　　　　　　1.　　　　　2.
telephone number.

Coin calls

Call the 800 number on the telephone _____.
　　　　　　　　　　　　　　　　　　　　3.
Follow the _____ on the telephone card.
　　　　　　4.

Card calls

_____ 911. Don't _____ 25 cents in the
5.　　　　　　　　　　　6.
telephone.

911 calls are free.

## ➤ Do it yourself! A plan-ahead project

**A. Discussion. Bring a phone card to class or use the
card here. Talk about the directions on the card.**

Press 1, the area code,
and the phone number.

**B. Pair work. Give your partner directions
to make a phone call with the card.**

**ABC**

Telephone Company

**Instructions:**
1. Call 1-800-555-8900.
2. Press 1, the area code, and the telephone number.
3. Press the calling card number. ▼

345-549-8222
Card number

**ABC**  Prepaid
Telephone
Calling Card

# Review

**A.** **Vocabulary. Write the names of the machines. Write <u>a</u> or <u>an</u>.**

1. _____

2. _____

3. _____

4. _____

**B.** **Conversation. Choose <u>your</u> response. Circle the letter.**

1. "Don't open the door."

   **a.** OK. No problem.          **b.** I don't know.

2. "Let's unplug the computer."

   **a.** OK.          **b.** How do I start the computer?

3. "How do I start the computer?"

   **a.** I don't know.          **b.** Good idea.

**C.** **Grammar. Write suggestions with <u>Let's</u>. Use the verbs from the box.**

| ~~call~~     read     press |
|---|

1. _Let's call the manager._ _____

2. _____

Directions
Close the lid.
Press START.

3. _____

**D.** **Reading and writing. Complete the directions.**

1. _____ the door.

2. _____ the <u>start</u> button.

3. _____ the <u>stop</u> button.

4. _____ the door.

**Microwave Oven Instructions**

## ➤ Do it yourself!

1. Point. Name the machines.

   *A copier*

2. What's wrong? Tell your partner.

   *The coffee maker is out of order.*

3. Create conversations for the people.

   *A: Press the off button.*
   *B: OK.*

4. Say more about the picture. Use your own words. Say as much as you can.

Now I can
- ❑ talk about machines.
- ❑ understand and give directions for machines.
- ❑ make suggestions.
- ❑ _____.

# Your customers

## ▶ Vocabulary

**Objectives**
Talk about
• colors and sizes
• problems with clothes
• likes and dislikes
• refunds and exchanges

### Picture dictionary

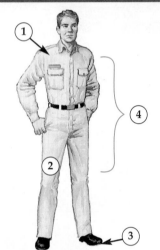

🎧 **A.** Listen.

| Clothes | | Colors | | Other words |
|---|---|---|---|---|
| ① a shirt | ⑥ a tie | ⑩ red | ⑭ black | ⑱ a customer |
| ② pants | ⑦ a dress | ⑪ blue | ⑮ green | ⑲ a salesperson |
| ③ a shoe | ⑧ a skirt | ⑫ yellow | ⑯ orange | ⑳ a receipt |
| ④ a uniform | ⑨ a jacket | ⑬ white | ⑰ brown | ㉑ a store |
| ⑤ a suit | | | | |

🎧 **B.** Listen again and repeat.

🎧 **C.** Now listen and point to the pictures.

**D.** Match the pictures and the words. Write the letter on the line.

1. __e__

2. _____

3. _____

4. _____

5. _____

6. _____

**a.** a green dress

**b.** an orange shirt

**c.** a blue shirt

**d.** an orange tie

**e.** a green uniform

**f.** a blue uniform

## ➤ Do it yourself!

**A.** Write about three classmates and their clothes.

Hi, I'm Tim.

| Name | Clothes |
|------|---------|
| Tim | black shoes, a white shirt, blue pants, an orange tie |
| 1. | |
| 2. | |
| 3. | |

**B. Pair work. Read your list of clothes. Your partner guesses the names.**

**Practical conversations**

**A.** Listen and read.

A: I need a uniform, please.
B: Sure. What size?
A: Small.
B: And what color?
A: Green.
B: OK. This way, please.

**B.** Listen again and repeat.

**C.** Pair work. **Now use your <u>own</u> words.**

A: I need _____, please.
B: _____. What size?
A: _____.
B: And what color?
A: _____.
B: _____. This way, please.

**Sizes**

small    medium    large

**A.** Listen and read.

A: Do you have this shirt in large?
B: Yes, we do.
A: Do you have these shoes in size 10?
B: No, we don't. I'm sorry.

**B.** Listen again and repeat.

**C.** Pair work. **Now use the pictures.**

A: Do you have this _____ in _____?
B: Yes, _____.

A: Do you have these _____ in _____?
B: No, _____. I'm sorry.

**this**

**these**

## A. Listen and read.

A: May I help you?

B: Yes, please. These pants are the wrong size.

A: Oh, I'm sorry. Do you have the receipt?

B: Yes, I think so.

## B. Listen again and repeat.

## C. Pair work. Now use your **own** problems.

A: May I help you?

B: Yes, please. These pants are _____.

A: Oh, I'm sorry. Do you have the receipt?

B: Yes, I think so.

**Problems with clothes**

the wrong size
the wrong color
too small
too large

## ➤ Do it yourself!

Pair work. **Create a conversation from the pictures. Use your own words.**

# Practical grammar

## The simple present tense: <u>have</u>, <u>want</u>, <u>need</u>, and <u>like</u>

I
You $\Big\}$ **need** a uniform.
We
They

I
You $\Big\}$ **don't need** a tie.
We
They

---

She **wants** the shirt.

She **likes** red shoes.

He **needs** a book.

Now he **has** a book.

She **doesn't need** a shirt. He **doesn't want** a new tie.

---

**A.** Complete each sentence with the simple present tense. Write the verb on the line.

1. I _____ a uniform, please.
   <u>need / needs</u>

2. We _____ that T-shirt in small.
   <u>have / has</u>

3. Marisol _____ black shoes.
   <u>want / wants</u>

4. I _____ this suit. It's too large.
   <u>don't like / doesn't like</u>

---

**Questions and short answers**

Do $\Big\{ \substack{you \\ they} \Big\}$ like this tie?   Yes, $\Big\{ \substack{I \\ we \\ they} \Big\}$ do.   No, $\Big\{ \substack{I \\ we \\ they} \Big\}$ don't.

Does $\Big\{ \substack{he \\ she \\ Bill} \Big\}$ like this tie?   Yes, $\Big\{ \substack{he \\ she \\ Bill} \Big\}$ does.   No, $\Big\{ \substack{he \\ she \\ Bill} \Big\}$ doesn't.

**Information questions**

What size do $\Big\{ \substack{you \\ they} \Big\}$ want?

---

**B.** Answer each question with a short answer.

1. Do you like green shoes? Yes, _____.

2. Do they have uniforms? Yes, _____.

3. Does Carlos need a tie? No, _____.

4. Does he want a blue suit? Yes, _____.

---

**Complete the questions. Choose words. Write the words on the line.**

1. _____ you _____ this new tie?
   <u>Do / Does</u>        <u>want / wants</u>

2. _____ she _____ a black skirt?
   <u>Do / Does</u>      <u>have / has</u>

3. What _____ they _____?
   <u>do / does</u>        <u>like / likes</u>

## This, that, these, those

I like **this** suit.

I like **that** suit.

I like **these** shoes.

I like **those** shoes.

**D.** **Look at the pictures. Complete the sentences. Use this, that, these, or those.**

1. I like __*this*__ uniform.

2. Please press _____ button.

3. We don't need more blue pants. We have _____ blue pants.

4. I want _____ shoes.

## ➤ Do it yourself!

**A.** **Pair work.** **Point. Ask and answer questions about the people.**

A:  Does she want the red dress?
B:  No. She wants the black dress.

**B.** **Personalization.** **Look at the picture. What do you like? Tell your partner.**

I like the computer.

**C.** **Tell the class about your partner.**

My partner likes the red dress.

**With words you know, (YOU) can talk to this customer.**

🎧 **A.** **Listen and read.**

**Customer:** Hi, I need some help. I need to return this microwave oven. It's too large.

(YOU) *I'm sorry. . . . Well, no problem. Do you have the receipt?*

**Customer:** Yes, I do. Here it is. Do you have any small microwaves?

(YOU) *Yes, I think so.*

**Customer:** Oh, that's good. Where are they?

(YOU) *They're across from the coffee makers.*

**Customer:** Great, thanks.

🎧 **B.** **Listen to the customer. Read <u>your</u> part.**

🎧 **C.** **Listen and read. Choose <u>your</u> response. Circle the letter.**

1. "Hi, I need some help."

   **a.** It's too large.　　　　　　**b.** Sure.

2. "These shirts are the wrong color."

   **a.** Oh, I'm sorry.　　　　　　**b.** That's good.

3. "Where are the computers?"

   **a.** This way, please.　　　　　**b.** They're from Japan.

🎧 **D.** **Listen. Choose <u>your</u> response. Circle the letter.**

1. **a.** Great, thanks.　　　　　　**b.** Sure, what size?

2. **a.** Yes, please.　　　　　　　**b.** Do you have the receipt?

3. **a.** OK. Are they too small?　　**b.** You're welcome.

🎧 **A.** Listen to the conversation. Read the form. Then circle the answer to the question.

**Peerless Uniform Company**

Customer's Name: _Oscar Soto_    **ORDER FORM**

**Uniform:** ❑ housekeeper   ☑ nurse   ❑ cook   ❑ bus driver

**Color:** ☑ green ❑ blue ❑ white ❑ black ❑ red ❑ yellow ❑ orange ❑ brown

| **Size:** | small | medium | large | extra large |
|---|---|---|---|---|
| Shirt | ❑ | ❑ | ☑ | ❑ |
| Pants | ❑ | ☑ | ❑ | ❑ |
| Skirt | ❑ | ❑ | ❑ | ❑ |

Who is talking to Mr. Soto?    **a.** a customer    **b.** a salesperson

🎧 **B.** Listen to the conversation. Then listen again and complete the order form.

**Peerless Uniform Company**

Customer's Name: _Martin Yu_    **ORDER FORM**

**Uniform:** ❑ housekeeper   ❑ nurse   ❑ cook   ❑ bus driver

**Color:** ❑ green ❑ blue ❑ white ❑ black ❑ red ❑ yellow ❑ orange ❑ brown

| **Size:** | small | medium | large | extra large |
|---|---|---|---|---|
| Shirt | ❑ | ❑ | ❑ | ❑ |
| Pants | ❑ | ❑ | ❑ | ❑ |
| Skirt | ❑ | ❑ | ❑ | ❑ |

## ➤ Do it yourself!

**A.** Write your <u>own</u> response. Then read your conversation out loud with a partner.

I have a problem. These pants are too small.

**YOU** _____

Here's my receipt.

**YOU** _____

I need some shoes. Could you please tell me where they are?

**YOU** _____

**B.** Discussion. Talk about a problem with clothes.

## Reading

**A.** Read the sign.

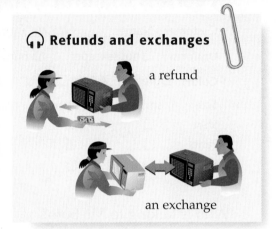

Refunds and exchanges

a refund

an exchange

**B.** Critical thinking. Read about these customers at Bell Office Supply. Choose a response for each customer.

 No problem.

 We don't give refunds. I'm sorry.

I'm sorry. You need a receipt.

Tanaka

1. Ella Tanaka wants a refund for a copier. She has the receipt.

   **Response:** _We don't give refunds. I'm sorry._

Gonzales

2. Pedro Gonzales wants to exchange copier paper. It's the wrong size. He has the receipt.

   **Response:** _____

Martinez

3. Alice Martinez wants to exchange a computer. She doesn't need the computer. She doesn't have the receipt.

   **Response:** _____

Gammon

4. John Gammon wants a refund for a coffee maker. He doesn't like the coffee maker. He has the receipt.

   **Response:** _____

**A.** Look at the return form. Then answer the questions.

**Bell Office Supply**

Exchange Department

Customer name: _____*Pedro Gonzales*_____

Item: _____*copier paper*_____

Reason for return: _____*wrong size*_____

1. What's the customer's name? _____

2. What does the customer want to return? _____

3. What's the problem? _____

**B.** Gregory Lin wants to exchange a red telephone. He wants a black telephone. Complete the return form for Mr. Lin.

**Bell Office Supply**

Exchange Department

Customer name: _____

Item: _____

Reason for return: _____

## ➤ Do it yourself!    A plan-ahead project

**Discussion. Bring receipts to class. Compare your receipts. Or use these receipts.**

What's the name of the store?

Does the store give refunds?

**Clothes & More**

Date Sept. 18/02

Name

Address

| Salesperson *Carol* | Cash X | Charge | Check |
|---|---|---|---|
| Quantity | Item | | Amount |
| 1 | Walking shorts - blue | | 29.95 |
| 1 | T-shirt, crew neck - white | | 12.00 |
| 1 | T-shirt, crew neck - black | | 12.00 |
| | All claims and returned goods MUST be accompanied by this bill. | | 53.95 |
| | | TAX | 2.26 |
| **Return Policy:** STORE CREDIT OR EXCHANGE ONLY. NO CASH OR CREDIT CARD REFUNDS. | | TOTAL | $56.21 |

**Ann's Closet**

Sold to

Address

| Sold By *Tom C* | Cash ✓ | C.O.D. | Charge | On Acct. | Mdse. Ret'd. | Paid Out |
|---|---|---|---|---|---|---|
| Qty. | | Description | | | Price | Amount |
| 1 | Shirt | | | | | 17.95 |
| 1 | Jacket | | | | | 22.95 |
| | 10% off | | | | | -4.09 |

FINAL SALE
NO REFUNDS,
EXCHANGE ONLY WITH RECEIPT.

| | Tax | 1.53 |
|---|---|---|
| | Total | $38.34 |

# Review

**A.** Vocabulary. **Match the picture with the words. Write the letter on the line.**

1. _____ old shoes

2. _____ a yellow uniform

3. _____ an old T-shirt

4. _____ a yellow skirt

a.

b.

c.

d.

**B.** Conversation. **Choose your response. Circle the letter.**

1. "I need a white shirt."

   **a.** OK. This way, please.          **b.** What color, please?

2. "Do you have these shoes in brown?"

   **a.** May I help you?          **b.** No, I'm sorry.

3. "These pants are the wrong size."

   **a.** Oh, I'm sorry.          **b.** Yes, we do.

**C.** Grammar. **Choose the verb. Write the verb on the line.**

1. Maria _____ large T-shirts.
   <br>like / likes

2. Ed _____ an old computer.
   <br>have / has

3. We _____ a new copier for the meeting room.
   <br>want / wants

4. The cashier _____ the key for the cash register.
   <br>doesn't have / don't have

**D.** Writing. **Return a coffee maker to Best Appliances. It's the wrong color. Complete the form.**

BEST APPLIANCES

Customer Service: Returns

Name: _____

Address: _____

Item you wish to return: _____

Reason for return: _____

> ## Do it yourself!

**1.** Point. Name the clothes.

*A yellow shirt*

**2.** Point. Ask questions.

*Do the students like those shirts?*

**3.** Create conversations for the people.

*A: May I help you?*
*B: Yes. This coffee maker is too small.*

**4.** Say more about the picture. Use your <u>own</u> words. Say as much as you can.

Now I can talk about
❑ colors and sizes.
❑ problems with clothes.
❑ likes and dislikes.
❑ refunds and exchanges.
❑ _____.

# Your time

**Objectives**
- tell time
- talk about days and dates
- read and write schedules

## ▶ Vocabulary

### Picture dictionary

(1)

(2) SECURITY BANK

(3)

(4)

(5)

(6) 2001 January S M T W T F S

(7) 2001 January S M T W T F S

(8) 2001 January S M T W T F S

(9) **Today is** **June 6, 2001**

(10) **Today is** **June 7, 2001**

### 🎧 A. Listen.

| <u>The time</u> | (6) <u>Months of the year</u> | | (7) <u>Days of the week</u> | | <u>Other words</u> |
|---|---|---|---|---|---|
| (1) 8:00 = eight o'clock | January | July | Sunday | Thursday | (8) a year |
| (2) 10:05 = ten-oh-five | February | August | Monday | Friday | (9) today |
| (3) 2:15 = two fifteen | March | September | Tuesday | Saturday | (10) tomorrow |
| (4) 11:30 = eleven thirty | April | October | Wednesday | | |
| (5) 6:45 = six forty-five | May | November | | | |
| | June | December | | | |

### 🎧 B. Listen again and repeat.

### 🎧 C. Now listen and point to the pictures.

## D. Match the clocks and the times. Write the letter on the line.

1. __b__

2. _____

3. _____

4. _____

5. _____

a. 12:00

b. 8:55

c. 4:15

d. 9:30

e. 11:45

## E. Read the time card and the receipt. Then answer the questions.

| TIME CARD | | IN | OUT |
|---|---|---|---|
| Tuesday | July 17, 2001 | 2:30 | |

1. What day is it?   *Tuesday*
2. What month is it?   _____
3. What year is it?   _____
4. What time is it?   _____

```
*************************************
       BEST SUPERMARKET
*************************************
Friday, August 9, 2002      7:15
Potatoes                  $1.99
Cheese                    $2.99
```

1. What day is it?   _____
2. What month is it?   _____
3. What year is it?   _____
4. What time is it?   _____

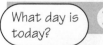

*What day is today?*

## ▶ Do it yourself!

*Sunday.*

### A. Answer the questions.

1. What day is today?   _____
2. What day is tomorrow?   _____
3. What month is it?   _____
4. What time is it right now?   _____

### B. Pair work. Check answers with your partner.

# Practical conversations

## Model 1 What time is it?

**A. Listen and read.**

> A: What time is it?
> B: It's 3:15.
> A: 3:15? Uh-oh. I'm late. Bye.
> B: Bye. See you later.

**B. Listen again and repeat.**

**C. Pair work. Now use real times.**

> A: What time is it?
> B: It's _____.
> A: _____? Uh-oh. I'm late. Bye.
> B: _____.

**More times**

9:00 a.m.    9:00 p.m.    noon    midnight

## Model 2 Ask about schedules.

**A. Listen and read.**

> A: When does school start?
> B: In September.
> A: And when does it end?
> B: In June.

**B. Listen again and repeat.**

**C. Pair work. Now ask about school and work.**

> A: When does _____ start?
> B: _____.
> A: And when does it end?
> B: _____.

**How to say it**

**in** September
**on** Wednesday
**at** 3:00
today
tomorrow

**A. Listen and read.**

A: What time does the post office open?
B: At 8:30 a.m.
A: And when does it close?
B: I'm not sure. At noon, I think.
A: At noon? That's great!

**B. Listen again and repeat.**

**C. Pair work. Now look at the signs. Talk about the places.**

A: What time does _____?
B: _____.
A: And when does it _____?
B: _____, I think.
A: At _____? That's great!

Union Supermarket
Open
7:00 AM to Midnight

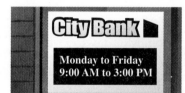

City Bank
Monday to Friday
9:00 AM to 3:00 PM

BROADWAY
Book Store
Noon to 9:00 PM

# ➤ Do it yourself!

**A. Personalization. Choose places in your neighborhood. Complete the signs for the places. Write opening and closing times.**

**B. Discussion. Talk about the places in your neighborhood.**

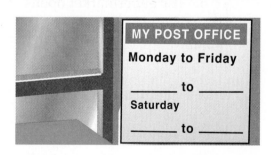

MY POST OFFICE
Monday to Friday
_____ to _____
Saturday
_____ to _____

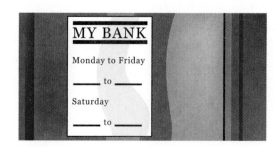

MY BANK
Monday to Friday
_____ to _____
Saturday
_____ to _____

MY SUPERMARKET
_____
_____
_____

## It's for days, dates, and times

It's Sunday.
It's 2002.
It's midnight.
It's 5:10.
Is it 4:15?          Yes, it is. / No, it isn't.

**A.** **Choose words. Write the words on the line.**

1. What day is it?     ___It's___ Monday.
   <small>Is / It's</small>

2. What time is it?     _____ 5:20.
   <small>Is / It's</small>

3. _____ April 15 or April 16?     Neither! It's April 17!
   <small>It is / Is it</small>

## Questions with <u>What time</u> and <u>When</u>

| | |
|---|---|
| **What time** does work start? | At 9:00. |
| **When** is the bank open? | From Monday to Friday. |
| **When** is the class? | At 6:50. |

**B.** **Write a question with <u>What time is</u> or <u>What time does</u>.**

1. **A:** _What time does the supermarket open?_____

   **B:** The supermarket opens at 7:30.

2. **A:** _____?

   **B:** It's 1:30.

**C.** **Write a question with <u>When is</u> or <u>When does</u>.**

1. **A:** _____?

   **B:** The restaurant closes at 11:00 p.m.

2. **A:** _____?

   **B:** The class is at 3:15.

**Write the date with a number.**

March **5**, 2000.

June **1**, 2003.

**Say the date with an ordinal number.**

"It's March **fifth**."

"It's June **first**."

**Ordinal numbers**

| | | |
|---|---|---|
| first | ninth | seventeenth |
| second | tenth | eighteenth |
| third | eleventh | nineteenth |
| fourth | twelfth | twentieth |
| fifth | thirteenth | twenty-first |
| sixth | fourteenth | twenty-second |
| seventh | fifteenth | thirtieth |
| eighth | sixteenth | thirty-first |

**D.** Read and listen to the ordinal numbers in the box. Then listen again and repeat.

**E.** Listen to the conversations. Then complete the dates.

1. March ___1___

2. October _____

3. April _____

4. August _____

**Say the dates out loud to a partner.**

➤ **Do it yourself!**

**A.** **Pair work. Ask questions about the picture. Use What time and When.**

A: *What time does the bank open?*

B: *9:00.*

**B.** **Personalization. Now talk to your partner about your supermarket.**

*My supermarket opens at 8:30 a.m.*

## Authentic practice 1

**With words you know, YOU can talk to this manager.**

### 🎧 A. Listen and read.

**Manager:** Good morning. Oh, it's 9:00.
You're right on time. That's great.

**YOU** *Thank you.*

**Manager:** Well, let me tell you a little about the job.
Your shift starts at 6:00.

**YOU** *6:00 a.m.?*

**Manager:** Well, actually no. At 6:00 p.m.

**YOU** *Good. No problem.*

**Manager:** Can you start this Tuesday, March 5?

**YOU** *I think so. . . . Yes, that's OK.*

**Manager:** Terrific! See you on Tuesday. Please be a
little early on your first day.

**YOU** *Sure. What time?*

**Manager:** How about 5:45?

**YOU** *OK.*

### 🎧 B. Listen to the manager. Read your part.

### 🎧 C. Listen and read. Choose your response. Circle the letter.

1. "You're a little early. That's good."

   **a.** Thanks.                    **b.** I'm sorry.

2. "Let me tell you a little about the job. Your shift starts at 6:00."

   **a.** I think so.                **b.** That's OK.

3. "Can you start on Tuesday, March 5?"

   **a.** No problem.                **b.** Press <u>start</u>.

### 🎧 D. Listen. Choose your response. Circle the letter.

1. **a.** Sure. What time does work start?    **b.** That's great.

2. **a.** Uh-oh. I'm late.                     **b.** Yes, sure.

3. **a.** OK.                                  **b.** I don't know.

**A.** Listen to the conversation. Then complete each sentence. Circle the letter.

1. The people are talking about _____.

   **a.** time and dates

   **b.** clothes and sizes

   **c.** buildings and places

2. The people are _____.

   **a.** a manager and a new employee

   **b.** a customer and a salesperson

   **c.** a student and a teacher

**B.** Listen to the conversation again. Circle Mr. Oakdale's start date and start time.

| Start date | Start time |
|------------|------------|
| May 18     | 8:15       |
| May 8      | 8:50       |

# ➤ Do it yourself!

**A.** Write your <u>own</u> response. Then read your conversation out loud with a partner.

 Can you start tomorrow on the 11:00 p.m. shift?

YOU _____

 On Mondays you need to be a little early. Is that OK for you?

YOU _____

 OK. See you this Monday at 10:00.

YOU _____

**B.** Discussion. Talk about the time work or school starts.

# Authentic practice 2

**A. Critical thinking.** Look at the work schedule and time card.
Is Claire Costello early, on time, or late?

| WORK SCHEDULE | WEEK OF *January 24* |
|---|---|
| **MONDAY** | *3:00 p.m.–9:00 p.m.* |
| **TUESDAY** | *7:00 a.m.–3:00 p.m.* |
| **WEDNESDAY** | *6:00 a.m.–2:00 p.m.* |
| **THURSDAY** | *3:00 p.m.–9:00 p.m.* |
| **FRIDAY** | *6:00 a.m.–12:00 noon* |

## Welcome Hotel

Name *Claire Costello*

### TIME CARD

| Day | | In |
|---|---|---|
| **MONDAY** | January 24 | 2:45 p.m. |
| **TUESDAY** | January 25 | 6:55 a.m. |
| **WEDNESDAY** | January 26 | 6:04 a.m. |
| **THURSDAY** | January 27 | 2:30 p.m. |
| **FRIDAY** | January 28 | 6:00 a.m. |

1. Monday, January 24     *early*

2. Tuesday, January 25     _____

3. Wednesday, January 26     _____

4. Thursday, January 27     _____

5. Friday, January 28     _____

**B. Critical thinking.** Claire Costello loves old
movies. She wants to see <u>King Kong</u>.
Look at the movie schedule.
Circle the times Claire can see <u>King Kong</u>.

# KING KONG

## ARTS THEATER
### MONDAY AND FRIDAY ONLY

Schedule of showings:
Monday 1/24:  6:00 p.m.,  8:00 p.m.,  10:30 p.m.
Friday 1/28:  4:45 p.m.,  7:30 p.m.,  midnight

Monday, January 24.

**A.** Look at Dan Kim's date book for March 17. Answer the questions.

1. What time does work start? _____

2. When does English class start? _____

**B.** Complete the date book for yourself. Write about this week.

MONDAY

TUESDAY

WEDNESDAY

THURSDAY

FRIDAY

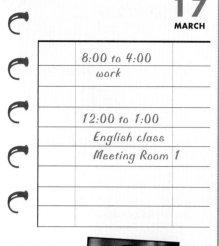

| 17 MARCH |
| --- |

| 8:00 to 4:00 work |
| 12:00 to 1:00 English class Meeting Room 1 |

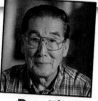

**Dan Kim**

> **Do it yourself!** A plan-ahead project

Discussion. **Bring a work schedule or a movie schedule to class. Or use the examples here and your date book from Exercise B. Talk about times and dates.**

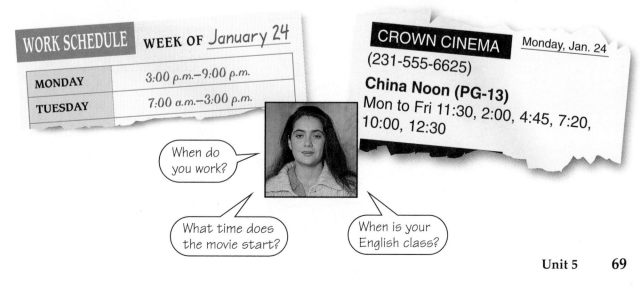

WORK SCHEDULE WEEK OF *January 24*

| MONDAY | 3:00 p.m.–9:00 p.m. |
| TUESDAY | 7:00 a.m.–3:00 p.m. |

CROWN CINEMA    Monday, Jan. 24
(231-555-6625)
**China Noon (PG-13)**
Mon to Fri 11:30, 2:00, 4:45, 7:20, 10:00, 12:30

When do you work?

What time does the movie start?

When is your English class?

**A.** Vocabulary. **Write the time with numbers.**

1. _____     2. _____     3. _____

**B.** Conversation. **Complete the conversations. Circle the letter.**

1. **A:** Bye.

   **B:** _____

   **a.** See you on Tuesday.        **b.** Oh, hi.

2. **A:** When does the movie start?

   **B:** _____

   **a.** On time.        **b.** At 4:30.

3. **A:** _____

   **B:** It's Thursday.

   **a.** What day is today?        **b.** What month is it?

**C.** Grammar. **Choose words. Write the words on the line.**

1. _____ 5:30?            2. _____ Monday.
   <sub>Is / Is it</sub>                 <sub>Is / It's</sub>

3. When _____ the English class?   4. What time _____?
   <sub>it's / is</sub>                          <sub>it's / is it</sub>

**D.** Reading. **Look at Paul Winston's date book and time card. On the time card circle the day he is late.**

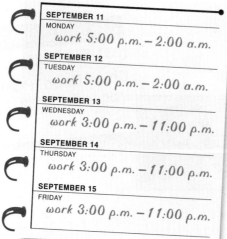

SEPTEMBER 11
MONDAY
work 5:00 p.m. – 2:00 a.m.

SEPTEMBER 12
TUESDAY
work 5:00 p.m. – 2:00 a.m.

SEPTEMBER 13
WEDNESDAY
work 3:00 p.m. – 11:00 p.m.

SEPTEMBER 14
THURSDAY
work 3:00 p.m. – 11:00 p.m.

SEPTEMBER 15
FRIDAY
work 3:00 p.m. – 11:00 p.m.

| TIME CARD | |
|---|---|
| Paul Winston | **IN** |
| Monday | 4:49 p.m. |
| Tuesday | 5:00 p.m. |
| Wednesday | 3:12 p.m. |
| Thursday | 2:55 p.m. |
| Friday | 3:00 p.m. |

> ▶ **Do it yourself!**
>
> **1.** Point. Talk about people and places.
>
>   *He's a bus driver.*
>   *The restaurant is next to the post office.*
>
> **2.** Create conversations for the people.
>
>   *A: What time is it?*
>   *B: It's 8:35.*
>
> **3.** Say more about the picture. Use your <u>own</u> words. Say as much as you can.

Now I can
- ❏ tell time.
- ❏ talk about days and dates.
- ❏ read and write schedules.
- ❏ _____.

# Your supplies and resources

 **Vocabulary**

**Objectives**
- talk about foods
- talk about likes and dislikes
- follow recipes

**Picture dictionary**

🎧 **A.** Listen.

<u>Foods and drinks</u>                                                                <u>Actions</u>

| | | | | |
|---|---|---|---|---|
| ① an apple ⟷ ② apples | ⑬ rice | ⑭ lettuce | ⑮ meat | ㉖ buy |
| ③ an onion ⟷ ④ onions | ⑯ chicken | ⑰ fish | ⑱ milk | ㉗ eat |
| ⑤ a carrot ⟷ ⑥ carrots | ⑲ bread | ⑳ cheese | ㉑ juice | |
| ⑦ a bean ⟷ ⑧ beans | ㉒ water | ㉓ coffee | | |
| ⑨ a tomato ⟷ ⑩ tomatoes | ㉔ tea | ㉕ sugar | | |
| ⑪ an egg ⟷ ⑫ eggs | | | | |

🎧 **B.** Listen again and repeat.

72      Unit 6

## C. Listen to the sentences. Look at the pictures.

a.  b.  c.

Now listen again. Write the letter of the picture on the line.

1. _____

2. _____

3. _____

## D. Collaborative activity. Work with a partner. Write a shopping list for this food.

1. _bread_  2. _____

3. _____  4. _carrots_

5. _____  6. _____

7. _____  8. _____

## ➤ Do it yourself!

## A. Ask your partner about foods. Complete the chart.

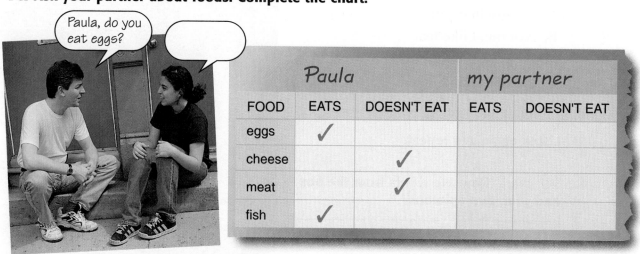

Paula, do you eat eggs?

| FOOD | Paula | | my partner | |
|------|-------|--|------------|--|
|  | EATS | DOESN'T EAT | EATS | DOESN'T EAT |
| eggs | ✓ | | | |
| cheese | | ✓ | | |
| meat | | ✓ | | |
| fish | ✓ | | | |

## B. Tell the class about your partner. Then tell the class about yourself.

My partner eats cheese. I don't eat eggs.

## Model 1 Talk about supplies you need.

**A.** Listen and read.

A: Hi, Tony. What's up?
B: Not much. But we need two boxes of rice.
A: Anything else?
B: No, that's all.

**B.** Listen again and repeat.

**C.** Pair work. **Now use the containers.**

A: Hi, _____. What's up?
B: Not much. But we need a _____.
A: Anything else?
B: No, that's all.

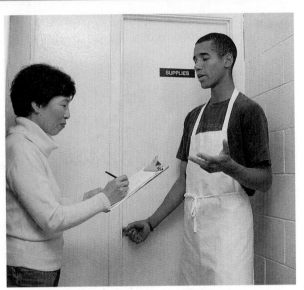

**Containers**

| a box of rice | a bottle of juice | a bag of onions | a can of coffee |

## Model 2 Talk about what you like. Agree and disagree.

**A.** Listen and read.

A: I really like coffee.
B: Not me. I like tea.
A: And what about milk?
B: I love milk.
A: Me too!

**B.** Listen again and repeat.

**C.** Pair work. **Now use words from the box and your <u>own</u> opinions.**

| juice | coffee | tea |
|-------|--------|-----|
| lettuce | tomatoes | onions |
| meat | fish | chicken |

**A:** I really like _____.

**B:** Not me. I like _____.

**A:** And what about _____?

**B:** I love _____.

**A:** Me too!

## Model 3  Ask about supplies.

 **A.** Listen and read.

**A:** Look in the supply room. Is there any juice?

**B:** Yes, there is.

**A:** And are there any onions?

**B:** No, there aren't. We're out of onions.

**B.** Listen again and repeat.

**C.** Pair work. **Now use the pictures.**

**A:** Look _____. Is there any _____?

**B:** Yes, there is.

**A:** And are there any _____?

**B:** No, there aren't. We're out of _____.

**How to say it**

in the refrigerator    on the shelf

**Is there any _____?**

**Are there any _____?**

## ➤ Do it yourself!

**Pair work. Create a conversation from the pictures. Talk about the supplies on the shelves.**

How many cans of coffee do we have?

## Count and non-count nouns

| Count nouns | Non-count nouns |
|---|---|
| a tomato    tomatoes<br>an apple    apples | milk<br>cheese |
| Count nouns use <u>a</u> and <u>an</u>.<br>Count nouns have plural forms. | Non-count nouns do not use <u>a</u> and <u>an</u>.<br>Non-count nouns do not have plural forms. |

**A.** Write these words in the lists.

| | | | |
|---|---|---|---|
| ~~apple~~ | ~~rice~~ | egg | meat |
| onion | carrot | cheese | tea |

**Count nouns**

1. _____apple_____

2. _____

3. _____

4. _____

**Non-count nouns**

1. _____rice_____

2. _____

3. _____

4. _____

---

**Questions with <u>How many</u> and <u>How much</u>**

Use <u>How many</u> to ask questions about count nouns.
   **How many** eggs do you want?

Use <u>How much</u> to ask questions about non-count nouns.
   **How much** milk do you want?

---

**B.** Choose <u>How many</u> or <u>How much</u>. Write the words on the line.

1. _____ sugar do you want?
   <small>How many / How much</small>

2. _____ lettuce do you have?
   <small>How many / How much</small>

3. _____ onions do you have in the refrigerator?
   <small>How many / How much</small>

4. _____ cans of beans do we have on the shelf?
   <small>How many / How much</small>

5. _____ rice do we need?
   <small>How many / How much</small>

## There is and There are

Use <u>There is</u> or <u>There's</u> with singular count nouns and all non-count nouns.
**There's** an **apple** on the shelf. (singular count noun)
**There's sugar** in this coffee. (non-count noun)

Use <u>There are</u> with plural nouns.
**There are** four **onions** in that bag.

**C.** **Choose <u>There's</u> or <u>There are</u>. Write the words on the line.**

1. _____ six carrots in that bag.
   There's / There are

2. _____ a tomato in the refrigerator.
   There's / There are

3. _____ five boxes of apples on the shelf.
   There's / There are

4. _____ bread in the supply room.
   There's / There are

---

**Questions with <u>Are there any</u> and <u>Is there any</u>**

**Are there any** onions on the shelf?     Yes, there are. / No, there aren't.
**Is there any** milk in this tea?     Yes, there is. / No, there isn't.

---

**D.** **Write questions with <u>Are there any</u> and <u>Is there any</u>.**

1. sugar / in the supply room? *Is there any sugar in the supply room?*

2. beans / in the kitchen? _____

3. cheese / on the shelf? _____

4. tomatoes / in the restaurant? _____

## ➤ Do it yourself!

**A.** **Pair work. Ask and answer questions about the picture. Use <u>Is there any</u> and <u>Are there any</u>.**

A: *Are there any eggs in this picture?*
B: *Yes, there are.*

**B.** **Personalization. Ask your partner questions about food and supplies. Use <u>How much</u> or <u>How many</u>.**

*How much juice do you have at home?*

**With words you know, YOU can talk to this grocer.**

**A. Listen and read.**

| | |
|---|---|
| **Grocer:** | Hi. How's it going? |
| **YOU** | *OK, Mr. Rossi. What do you need today?* |
| **Grocer:** | Well, let's start with a case of eggs. |
| **YOU** | *OK. One case of eggs.* |
| **Grocer:** | Actually, let's make that two cases of eggs, one large and one medium. |
| **YOU** | *Two cases of eggs. What about tomatoes?* |
| **Grocer:** | I'll take two boxes of those tomatoes from Mexico. |
| **YOU** | *OK. Anything else?* |
| **Grocer:** | No, I think that's all for today. |
| **YOU** | *OK. Great, Mr. Rossi. Thanks.* |

**B. Listen to the grocer. Read your part.**

**C. Listen and read. Choose your response. Circle the letter.**

1. "I need to buy a box of large tomatoes."

   **a.** One box of large tomatoes. OK.    **b.** I don't know.

2. "Let's start with coffee. Do you have any from Brazil?"

   **a.** Do you like milk in your coffee?    **b.** Yes, I think so.

3. "I think that's all for now."

   **a.** OK. See you later.    **b.** Anything else?

**D. Listen. Choose your response. Circle the letter.**

1. **a.** Yes, there is.    **b.** Do you want large or medium?

2. **a.** Not much.    **b.** How many boxes do you want?

3. **a.** OK. What do you want today?    **b.** How about rice?

## Listening comprehension

**A. Listen to the conversations. Then answer the questions. Circle the letter.**

1. What's Jean's occupation?    **a.** cook    **b.** cashier
2. Where are the two people?    **a.** in a kitchen    **b.** at the office

**B. Read the list of foods. Then listen to Conversation 1 again. Check ☑ the foods that are in the Super Salad.**

❑ beans ❑ lettuce ❑ tomatoes ❑ onions ❑ chicken ❑ cheese

**C. Look at the pictures of the three sandwiches. Listen to Conversation 2 again.**

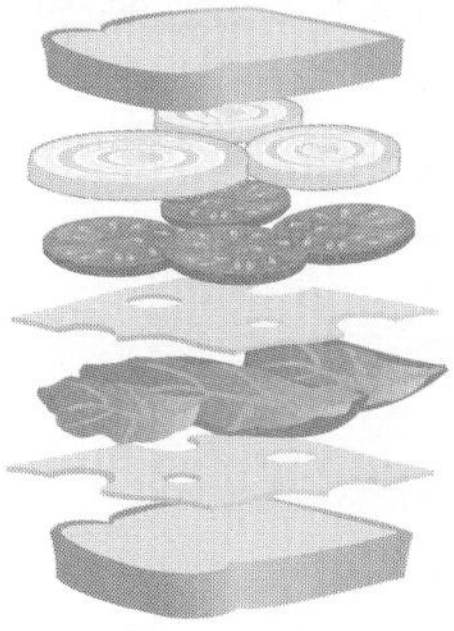

a.

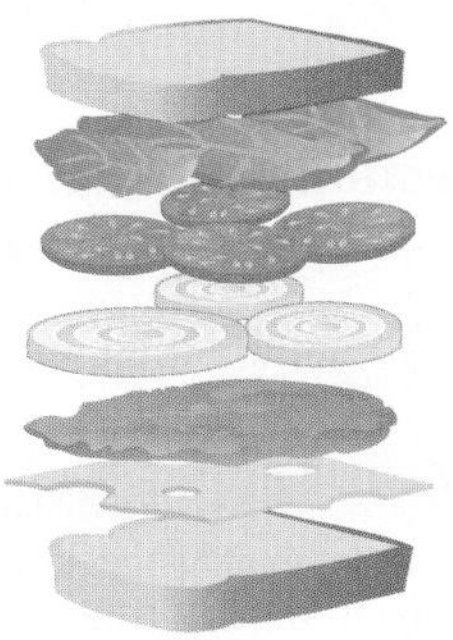

b.

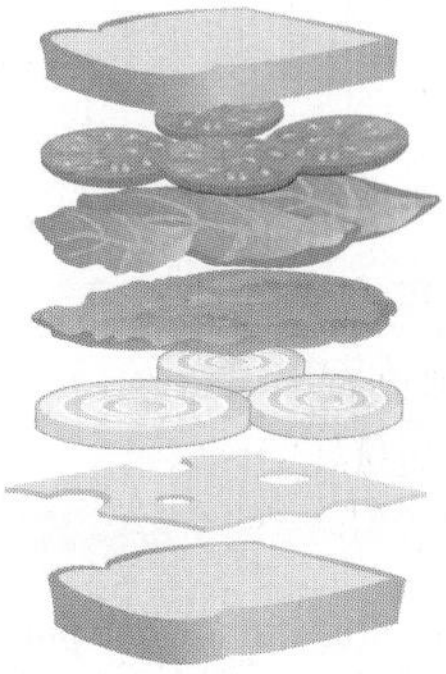

c.

**Now listen again. Circle the letter of the sandwich in the conversation.**

## Do it yourself!

**A. Write your <u>own</u> response. Then read your conversation out loud with a partner.**

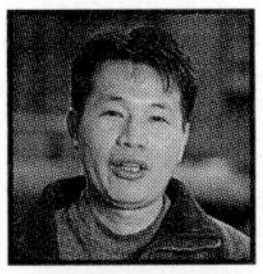

We need bread. Please buy some when you're at the store.

YOU ______________________________

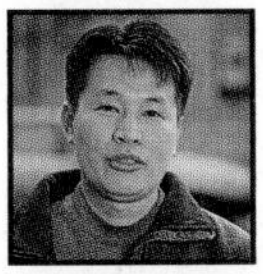

Do you think we need anything else?

YOU ______________________________

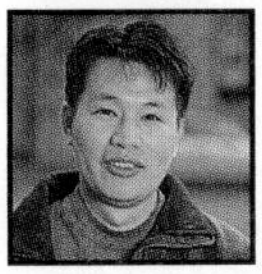

OK. See you later. Thanks.

YOU ______________________________

**B. Discussion. Talk about supplies you need or about foods you really like.**

## Reading

**A. Look at the box. What do you need to cook spaghetti?**

☐ water ☐ oil

☐ salt ☐ onions

☐ spaghetti ☐ sugar

**B. Critical thinking. Are the directions correct? Write <u>yes</u> or <u>no</u>.**

| 1 Put water in the pot. | 2 Put 1 tablespoon of oil and 1 teaspoon of salt in the pot. | 3 Boil the water. |
| --- | --- | --- |
| 4 Put the spaghetti in the boiling water. | 5 Cook the spaghetti for 10 minutes. | 6 Drain the spaghetti. |

1.  Put the spaghetti in the pot. Then boil the water. __no__

2.  Cook the spaghetti. Then drain the spaghetti. _____

3.  Put the water, salt, and oil in the pot. Then boil the water. _____

4.  Drain the spaghetti. Then boil the water. _____

**C. Pair work. Tell your partner how to cook spaghetti.**

First, put water in a large pot.

**A.** Read the recipe for tomato bean soup.

## Tomato Bean Soup

<u>Ingredients</u>

| | |
|---|---|
| 1 medium onion | 2 cups of water |
| 2 large carrots | 2 15-ounce cans of tomatoes |
| 1 tablespoon of oil | 1 10-ounce can of small white beans |

<u>Directions</u>

1. Chop the onion and carrots. Put the onion, carrots, and oil in a large pot. Cook for five minutes.
2. Put the water in the pot. Put the tomatoes in the pot. Cook for 30 minutes.
3. Put the beans in the pot. Cook for 10 minutes.

🎧 **Recipe words**

chop

a cup

**B.** Critical thinking. **Raquel Taylor wants to make tomato bean soup. What does she need? Look at the picture of the foods she has in her kitchen. Write a shopping list for her.**

*Shopping List*

## ➤ Do it yourself!    A plan-ahead project

**A.** Discussion. **Bring your own recipes to class. Talk about the recipes. Or use this recipe.**

**B.** Collaborative activity. **Work with a partner. Choose a recipe you like. Make a shopping list for that recipe.**

Shopping List

apples

## Fruit Salad

<u>Ingredients</u>

| | |
|---|---|
| Apples | Oranges |
| Pears | Bananas |

<u>Directions</u>

Cut the fruit in small pieces.
Put the fruit in a large bowl.
Serve and enjoy.

**A.** Vocabulary. **Write a shopping list for the foods in the picture.**

*shopping List*

**B.** Conversation. **Choose <u>your</u> response. Circle the letter.**

1. "Are we out of onions?"

   **a.** No, there's a bag on the shelf.     **b.** Not me.

2. "We need milk."

   **a.** How much do you want?     **b.** See you tomorrow.

3. "Do you need anything else?"

   **a.** Yes, I want bread, please.     **b.** Yes, me too.

**C.** Grammar. **Choose words. Write the words on the line.**

1. _____ coffee in this can.
   <br>There's / There are

2. _____ two bags of rice in the supply room.
   <br>There's / There are

3. _____ any juice in the refrigerator?
   <br>Is there / Are there

4. _____ apples do we need?
   <br>How much / How many

**D.** Reading. **Match the pictures with the directions. Write the letters on the lines.**

a.     b.     c.     d.

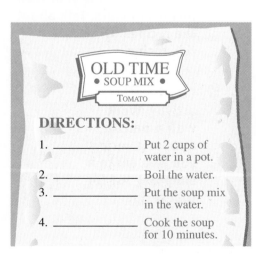

OLD TIME
• SOUP MIX •
TOMATO

**DIRECTIONS:**

1. _____ Put 2 cups of water in a pot.
2. _____ Boil the water.
3. _____ Put the soup mix in the water.
4. _____ Cook the soup for 10 minutes.

## ➤ Do it yourself!

1. Point. Name the foods and drinks.
   *Onions*

2. Point. Ask questions.
   *How much juice does he have?*

3. Create conversations for the people.
   *A: Where's the coffee?*
   *B: In Aisle 2.*

4. Say more about the picture. Use your <u>own</u> words. Say as much as you can.

**AISLE 2**

Now I can
☐ talk about foods.
☐ talk about likes and dislikes.
☐ follow recipes.
☐ _____.

# Your relationships

## ➤ Vocabulary

### Picture dictionary

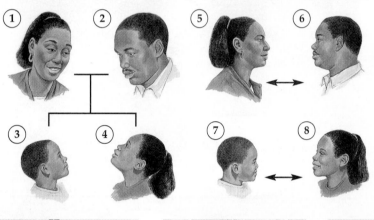

🎧 **A.** Listen.

**Relationships**

| | | | |
|---|---|---|---|
| ① a mother | ⑤ a wife | | |
| ② a father | ⑥ a husband | | |
| ③ a son | ⑦ a brother | | |
| ④ a daughter | ⑧ a sister | | |
| | ⑨ friends | | |

**Actions**

| | |
|---|---|
| ⑩ fix | ⑮ stay home |
| ⑪ install | ⑯ study |
| ⑫ drive | ⑰ come |
| ⑬ clean | ⑱ go |
| ⑭ work | |

🎧 **B.** Listen again and repeat.

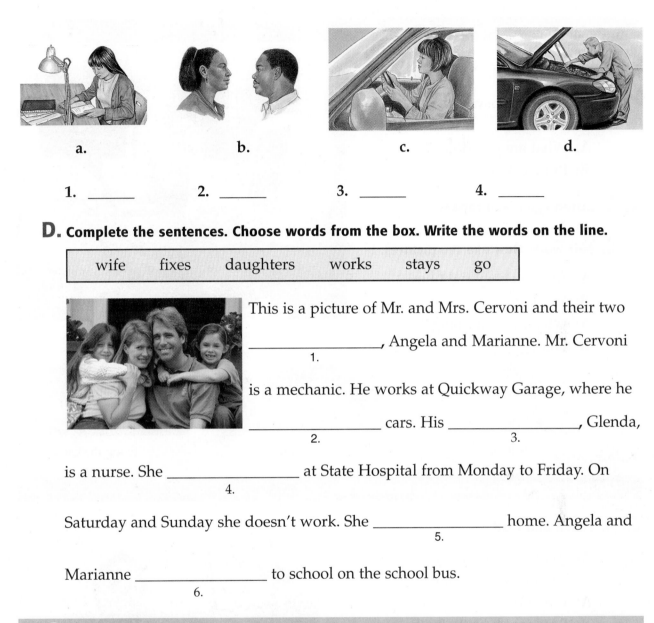

**C.** Look at the pictures. Listen to the sentences. Then listen again.
Match the pictures and the sentences. Write the letter on the line.

a.　　　　　b.　　　　　c.　　　　　d.

1. _____　　2. _____　　3. _____　　4. _____

**D.** Complete the sentences. Choose words from the box. Write the words on the line.

| wife | fixes | daughters | works | stays | go |
|------|-------|-----------|-------|-------|-----|

This is a picture of Mr. and Mrs. Cervoni and their two

_____, Angela and Marianne. Mr. Cervoni
　　　　　1.

is a mechanic. He works at Quickway Garage, where he

_____ cars. His _____, Glenda,
　　　　2.　　　　　　　　　　　　　　3.

is a nurse. She _____ at State Hospital from Monday to Friday. On
　　　　　　　　4.

Saturday and Sunday she doesn't work. She _____ home. Angela and
　　　　　　　　　　　　　　　　　　　　5.

Marianne _____ to school on the school bus.
　　　　　6.

## ➤ Do it yourself!

**A.** Complete the chart. Write about two friends or two people in your family.

| Name | Relationship | Occupation | Workplace |
|------|--------------|------------|-----------|
| Dan | brother | cook | restaurant |
| 1. | | | |
| 2. | | | |

**B.** Tell the class about your friends or family.

*Dan is my brother. He's a cook. He works in a restaurant.*

**Practical conversations**

**A.** Listen and read.

A: Are you busy right now?
B: Yes, I am.
A: What are you doing?
B: I'm working.

**B.** Listen again and repeat.

**C.** Pair work. **Now use the pictures.**

A: Are you busy right now?
B: Yes, I am.
A: What are you doing?
B: I'm _____.

cleaning

studying

fixing the car

**A.** Listen and read.

A: Are you ready to go?
B: No, I'm sorry. Not yet.
A: Why not?
B: Because I have to fix the computer.
A: OK.

**B.** Listen again and repeat.

**C.** Pair work. **Now use your <u>own</u> words.**

A: Are you ready to go?
B: No, I'm sorry. Not yet.
A: Why not?
B: Because I have to _____.
A: _____.

**A. Listen and read.**

A: Can John clean the meeting room?

B: No, I'm sorry. He can't.

A: Why?

B: Because he's at the post office right now.

A: Well, when can he clean the meeting room?

B: In an hour.

**B. Listen again and repeat.**

**C.** Pair work. **Now use actions from the box and your _own_ words.**

| install the telephones | clean the kitchen | fix the computer |
|---|---|---|

A: Can _____?

B: No, I'm sorry. _____ can't.

A: Why?

B: Because _____.

A: Well, when can _____?

B: In _____.

**⌒ How to say it**

in an hour     in 10 minutes

## ➤ Do it yourself!

Pair work. **Continue the conversation for the people in the picture.**

Are you ready to eat?

**Practical grammar**

| | | |
|---|---|---|
| Use the present continuous to talk about right now. | **Questions** | **Answers** |
| **A:** What **are** you **doing** right now? | **Is** he **fixing** the bus? | Yes, he is. / No, he's not. |
| **B:** I'm busy. I'm **working**. | | |
| | **Are** you **studying** English? | Yes, I am. / No, I'm not. |

I'm
You're
He's
She's } **working**.

We're
You're
They're } **working**.

**A. Choose a word. Write the word on the line.**

1. _____ Pedro fixing the lawn mower?
   <u>Is / Are</u>

2. Is Lana _____ that book?
   <u>read / reading</u>

3. What _____ they doing now?
   <u>is / are</u>

4. Who's _____ room 22?
   <u>clean / cleaning</u>

5. Are you _____ the shelves in the kitchen or the supply room?
   <u>install / installing</u>

**B. Complete each sentence with the present continuous. Write the words on the line.**

1. I'm busy. I _____.
   <u>work</u>

2. Rafael can't clean the meeting room. He _____ the telephones.
   <u>fix</u>

3. We're not ready. We _____ the kitchen.
   <u>clean</u>

| | | |
|---|---|---|
| He **can fix** copiers. He **can't fix** cars. | **Questions** | **Answers** |
| | Can you go tomorrow? | Yes, I can. / No, I can't. |
| | What can you do? | I can write recipes. |
| | Who can help my friend? | Al can. |
| Don't use <u>to</u> with <u>can</u>: I can drive. | | |

**Ask your partner these questions. Then write about your partner.**

1. Can you drive?

2. What can you fix?

1. My partner _____.

2. My partner _____.

## Have to and don't have to

She **has to work** on Monday.

MONDAY

She **doesn't have to work** on Sunday.

SUNDAY

Do you have to return that uniform?          Yes, I do. / No, I don't.

Why does Juan have to work on Sunday?        Because he can't work on Monday.

**D.** **Choose have to or has to. Write the words on the line.**

1. I _____ start the coffee maker in 10 minutes. Do you have that can of coffee?
   have to / has to

2. Who _____ clean the shelves in the supply room? Is it you or Gonzalo?
   have to / has to

3. Why do you _____ call the store? Is that paper the wrong color?
   have to / has to

4. The electricians don't _____ install the copiers today. Tomorrow's OK.
   have to / has to

## ➤ Do it yourself!

**A.** **Personalization.**
**Complete your date book for next week.**

MONDAY
*go to the supermarket*

**B.** **Pair work.**
**Ask and answer questions about your schedule.**

Can you go to the movies on Friday?

No, I can't. I have to work on Friday.

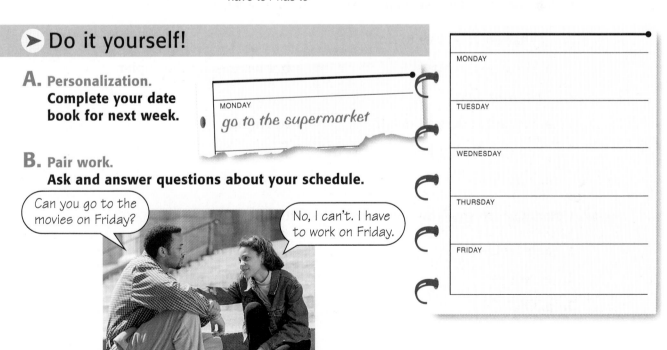

MONDAY

TUESDAY

WEDNESDAY

THURSDAY

FRIDAY

Unit 7     89

# Authentic practice 1

**With words you know, YOU can talk to this manager.**

## 🎧 A. Listen and read.

**Manager:** I know you don't work on Saturdays, but do you think you could work tomorrow? Tom's taking a personal day because his son is in the hospital.

**YOU** *Oh, I'm sorry. . . . No problem. I can work tomorrow. What do you need?*

**Manager:** Someone has to install the new telephones in the King Street building. You can do that, can't you?

**YOU** *Sure. I can install telephones.*

**Manager:** That's great! See you tomorrow, then. And thanks a million.

**YOU** *You're welcome.*

## 🎧 B. Listen to the manager. Read your part.

## 🎧 C. Listen and read. Choose your response. Circle the letter.

1. "What do you have to do?"

   **a.** Because I'm busy.                    **b.** I have to fix the copier.

2. "Are you busy?"

   **a.** No. What do you need?               **b.** Thanks.

3. "You can do that later, can't you?"

   **a.** Yes, I can.                          **b.** Not yet.

## 🎧 D. Listen. Choose your response. Circle the letter.

1. **a.** Is he OK?                            **b.** I'm too busy right now.

2. **a.** Not yet.                             **b.** No, I'm sorry. I can't.

3. **a.** OK.                                  **b.** Not me.

90    Unit 7

🎧 **A. Listen to the conversation. Then complete the sentences. Circle the letter.**

1. The two people are _____.

   **a.** a husband and a wife          **b.** an employee and a manager

2. They're talking about _____.

   **a.** a personal day          **b.** supplies

🎧 **B. Read the sentences. Then listen again. Complete each sentence with <u>Claire</u> or <u>Boris</u>.**

1. _____ has to take a personal day.

2. _____ has to buy a car.

3. _____ has to install the exit doors.

4. _____ can clean the meeting rooms at 6:00.

🎧 **C. Discussion. Listen again. Talk about Boris's problem. Use the pictures and your <u>own</u> words.**

## ➤ Do it yourself!

**A. Write your <u>own</u> response. Then read your conversation out loud with a partner.**

 Are you very busy right now?

YOU _____

 I need some help.

YOU _____

 I need someone to take these supplies to the office. Can you do that?

YOU _____

**B. Discussion. Talk about what you have to do at work or at home.**

## Reading

**A.** Read the personal day policy from the Quality Paint Company.

**Quality Paint Company**

Personal Day Policy

Every employee is entitled to 4 paid personal days a year. When you can't come to work, you MUST:

- Call or speak to your manager one day BEFORE the personal day.
  **For example:** If you need to take a personal day on Wednesday, you have to tell your manager on Tuesday.

- Tell your manager the date you can return to work.
- Fill out a personal day form when you return to work.

**B.** Critical thinking. **Read about these employees of the Quality Paint Company. Are they following the company policy for personal days? Write yes or no.**

Hakeem

1. Michael Hakeem has to buy a new car. On Monday morning, he tells his manager he can't come to work on Tuesday, March 13. On Wednesday, when he returns, he fills out a personal day form. _____

Johnson

2. On Wednesday, March 14, Lucy Johnson can't go to work. She doesn't tell her manager. She stays home. When she returns on Thursday, she fills out the personal day form. _____

Lara

3. Today is Friday, March 15. Andrea Lara tells her manager she can't come to work next week. When Andrea returns, she fills out a personal day form for five days. _____

**A.** Read Renee Samadi's personal day form. Then read the sentences. Write <u>yes</u> or <u>no</u>.

*Quality Paint Company*

**Personal Day Form**

Employee: _____Renee Samadi_____    Department: _____Quality Control_____

Date(s) of absence: _____May 22_____    Date of return to work: _____May 23_____

Reason: _____My husband is very sick. I have to take my husband to the doctor._____

1. Renee Samadi's personal day is May 23. _____

2. Renee Samadi works in the Quality Control Department. _____

3. Renee Samadi's husband needs to go to the doctor. _____

**B.** Read about Michael Hakeem again in Exercise B on page 92. Mr. Hakeem works in the Sales Department. Fill out his personal day form.

*Quality Paint Company*

**Personal Day Form**

Employee: _____    Department: _____

Date(s) of absence: _____    Date of return to work: _____

Reason: _____

➤ Do it yourself!

Take a personal day. Complete the personal day form for yourself.

*Quality Paint Company*

**Personal Day Form**

Employee: _____    Department: _____Customer Service_____

Date(s) of absence: _____    Date of return to work: _____

Reason: _____

## Review

**A. Vocabulary. Choose words to complete the sentences. Write the words on the line.**

Marie and Paul Martin have a _____, Peter, and a daughter, Nicole. Paul

             1. husband / son

is the father, and Marie is the _____. Marie _____ at the North

           2. mother / daughter          3. installs / works

Side Hospital. She is a nurse. Tomorrow Marie is _____, and she can't go to

                             4. busy / ready

work. She _____ take a personal day.

        5. has / has to

**B. Conversation. Choose <u>your</u> response. Circle the letter.**

1. "When can you go to the supply room?"

   **a.** In 15 minutes.             **b.** Because I'm too busy.

2. "Why are you late today?"

   **a.** In an hour.             **b.** Because my husband is in the hospital.

3. "What are you doing now?"

   **a.** I'm working.             **b.** I'm ready.

**C. Grammar. Choose words. Write the words on the line.**

1. Who _____ this bus? Walter?

        driving / is driving

2. I can't clean the office now. I _____ go to the bank.

                   have to / don't have to

3. Can you _____ to the supermarket? We're out of milk.

         to go / go

**D. Reading. Read the personal day form. Then write <u>yes</u>, <u>no</u>, or <u>I don't know</u>.**

**Galaxy Garden Supplies** _____ **Personal Day Form**

Employee: ___Valerie Lavin___

Today's date: ___August 3___      Date(s) of absence: ___August 4___

Reason: ___My son has to go to the doctor._____

1. The employee is Valerie Lavin's son. _____

2. The personal day is August 4. _____

3. Valerie has a daughter. _____

## ➤ Do it yourself!

**1.** Point. Name the relationships.
*Father, daughter*

**2.** Point. What are the people doing?
*She's studying.*

**3.** Create conversations for the people.
*A: What are you doing?*
*B: I'm fixing the door.*

**4.** Say more about the picture. Use your <u>own</u> words. Say as much as you can.

Now I can
☐ talk about what I'm doing.
☐ talk about what I can do.
☐ talk about what I have to do.
☐ tell people why.
☐ _____.

# Your health and safety

 **Vocabulary**

**Objectives**

- talk about accidents
- talk about health
- call 911
- make an appointment

**Picture dictionary**

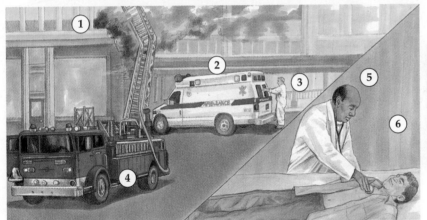

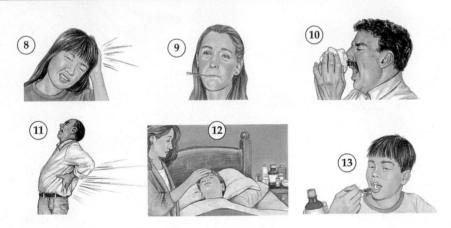

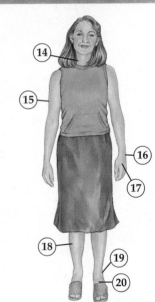

🎧 **A.** **Listen.**

**Health and safety**

| | | | |
|---|---|---|---|
| ① a fire | ⑥ an emergency room | ⑩ have a cold |
| ② an ambulance | ⑦ an accident | ⑪ have a backache |
| ③ a paramedic | ⑧ have a headache | ⑫ have the flu |
| ④ a fire truck | ⑨ have a fever | ⑬ take medicine |
| ⑤ a doctor | | |

**Parts of the body**

| | |
|---|---|
| ⑭ a neck | ⑱ a leg |
| ⑮ an arm | ⑲ an ankle |
| ⑯ a wrist | ⑳ a foot |
| ⑰ a hand | |

🎧 **B.** **Listen again and repeat.**

**C.** Listen to the conversations. What's the problem? Circle the letter.

1. a.     b.

2. a.     b.

3. a.    b.

**D.** Choose words. Write the words on the line.

1. Linda hurt her _____, and now she can't write.
   <u>foot / hand</u>

2. Ms. Yin hurt her back. She has to go to _____.
   <u>the doctor / the accident</u>

3. Mr. Ortiz has the flu. He has to take _____.
   <u>medicine / an ambulance</u>

4. There's _____ on Park Avenue. Call a fire truck!
   <u>a fire / a doctor</u>

> ➤ **Do it yourself!**

**A.** Read the health problems. Then complete the chart.

> When I have a cold, I eat chicken soup and I drink tea.

| Problem | Medicine | Foods | Drinks |
|---|---|---|---|
| a cold | I take aspirin. | I eat chicken soup. | I drink tea. |
| a backache | | | |
| the flu | | | |
| a headache | | | |

**B.** Discussion. Talk about the health problems and what you do.

## Practical conversations

---

### Model 1    Make a phone call.

🎧 **A.** **Listen and read.**

> **A:** Hello?
> **B:** Hi, Dan. This is Bill. Can you talk?
> **A:** Well, I'm fixing a door right now.
>     I'm sorry. Can I call you back?
> **B:** Sure. No problem. Talk to you later.
> **A:** Thanks. Bye.
> **B:** Bye.

🎧 **B.** **Listen again and repeat.**

**C.** **Pair work.** **Now use your <u>own</u> words.**

> **A:** Hello?
> **B:** Hi, _____. This is _____. Can you talk?
> **A:** Well, I'm _____ right now. I'm sorry. Can I call you back?
> **B:** Sure. No problem. Talk to you later.
> **A:** Thanks. Bye.
> **B:** Bye.

---

### Model 2    Make an appointment.

🎧 **A.** **Listen and read.**

> **A:** Doctor Baker's office. How can I help you?
> **B:** This is Dan Kim. I need to make an
>     appointment. I hurt my back.
> **A:** Oh, I'm sorry. How about tomorrow at 9:30?
> **B:** Tomorrow at 9:30? That's fine. See you then.
> **A:** Feel better!
> **B:** Thanks a lot.

🎧 **B.** **Listen again and repeat.**

**C.** Pair work. **Now use your <u>own</u> words.**

**A:** Doctor _____ 's office. How can I help you?

**B:** I need to make an appointment. I _____.

**A:** Oh, I'm sorry. How about _____ at _____?

**B:** _____? That's fine. See you then.

**A:** Feel better!

**B:** _____.

---

**Model 3    Make a 911 call.**

🎧 **A.** **Listen and read.**

**A:** This is 911.

**B:** There's an accident at the corner of Front Street and Third Avenue.

**A:** Do you need an ambulance or a fire truck?

**B:** An ambulance, please.

**A:** OK. It's on its way.

🎧 **B.** **Listen again and repeat.**

**C.** Pair work. **Now use your <u>own</u> words.**

**A:** This is 911.

**B:** There's _____ at _____.

**A:** Do you need _____?

**B:** _____.

---

➤ **Do it yourself!**

Pair work. **Create a conversation from the pictures. Use your <u>own</u> words.**

# Practical grammar

## Possessives

Is this **your** coffee?

No, it's **John's** coffee.

| I'm | | | my | |
|---|---|---|---|---|
| You're | | | your | |
| He's | | | his | |
| She's | fixing | | her | car. |
| We're | | | our | |
| You're | | | your | |
| They're | | | their | |

**A.** Choose words. Write the words on the line.

1. This is my daughter, and _____ name is Sonia.
   his / her

2. I have to call Shardul and Clara. Do you have _____ phone number?
   his / their

3. He has two offices. _____ new office is on Smith Street.
   His / Their

4. This is _____ old uniform. It's too small.
   Fran / Fran's

## Never, sometimes, always

| 0% | | 100% |
|---|---|---|
| **never** | sometimes | **always** |

Use the simple present tense with <u>never</u>, <u>sometimes</u>, and <u>always</u>.
   I **sometimes drink** coffee.
<u>Never</u>, <u>sometimes</u>, and <u>always</u> go before the simple present tense verb.
   I **never drink** tea.
<u>Never</u>, <u>sometimes</u>, and <u>always</u> go after forms of the verb <u>be</u>.
   I'**m never** busy.

**B.** Answer the questions. Use <u>never</u>, <u>sometimes</u>, or <u>always</u>.

1. What do you take when you have a headache? *I always take aspirin.*

2. Do you drink tea? _____

3. Are you busy on Saturdays? _____

4. Do you go to the emergency room when you have the flu? _____

Use the simple present tense with <u>have</u>, <u>want</u>, <u>need</u>, and <u>like</u>.
I **like** that store.
Use the simple present tense with <u>never</u>, <u>sometimes</u>, and <u>always</u>.
I always **eat** early.

Don't use the present continuous with <u>never</u>, <u>sometimes</u>, and <u>always</u>.
Use the present continuous to talk about what you are doing right now.
What are you doing? I'**m talking** to the doctor.

**C.** **Choose the present continuous or the simple present tense. Write the words on the line.**

1. Mario _____ a backache.
   has / is having

2. He always _____ that bus.
   drives / is driving

3. Do you _____ an ambulance?
   need / needing

4. I'm _____ the doctor right now.
   call / calling

**D.** **Complete the chart about yourself and a friend or a family member. Then tell the class about one person.**

I always have headaches.

| Name | Has colds | Has headaches | Takes medicine |
|------|-----------|---------------|----------------|
| Tasha | never | sometimes | sometimes |
| 1. | | | |
| 2. | | | |

➤ **Do it yourself!**

**Point. Talk about the picture.**

*He hurt his arm. He hurt his head.*

**With words you know, YOU can talk to this nurse.**

🎧 **A.** **Listen and read.**

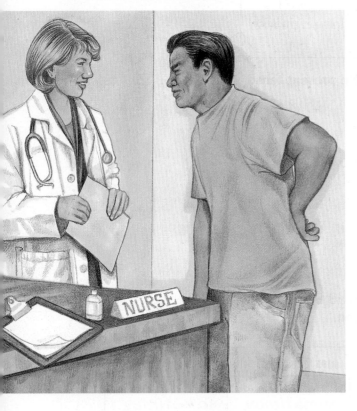

**Nurse:** How can I help you?

**YOU** *I hurt my back at work.*

**Nurse:** Oh, I'm sorry. Does it hurt anywhere else? What about down your leg?

**YOU** *Down my leg? Yes. Down my right leg.*

**Nurse:** Well, a doctor can see you in about an hour. First, let me give you some medicine. Can you take aspirin?

**YOU** *Yes. I always take aspirin.*

**Nurse:** OK, take these two aspirins. Have a seat, and please fill out this form. And I hope you feel better soon.

**YOU** *Thanks a lot.*

🎧 **B.** **Listen to the nurse. Read your part.**

🎧 **C.** **Listen and read. Choose your response. Circle the letter.**

1. "How can I help you?"

   **a.** Not me.   **b.** I need to see the doctor.

2. "What's the problem?"

   **a.** I hurt my right arm.   **b.** That's OK.

3. "Feel better soon."

   **a.** Thank you.   **b.** You're welcome.

🎧 **D.** **Listen. Choose your response. Circle the letter.**

1. **a.** Yes, sure. It hurts here.   **b.** Dr. Smith's office.

2. **a.** Yes, I can. Thank you.   **b.** Can I call you back?

3. **a.** Me too.   **b.** OK, thanks.

🎧 **A.** **Listen to the conversation. Then complete the sentences. Circle the letter.**

1. The women are _____.

   **a.** on the telephone      **b.** in a van

2. They are _____.

   **a.** doctors      **b.** friends

🎧 **B.** **Read the questions. Then listen again. Listen for numbers in the conversation. Circle the letter.**

1. What time was the accident?

   **a.** 8:30      **b.** 9:00

2. How many people were in the van?

   **a.** 1      **b.** 3

3. How many people in the van were hurt?

   **a.** 2      **b.** 3

4. How many paramedics were in the ambulance?

   **a.** 1      **b.** 2

## ➤ Do it yourself!

**A.** **Write your __own__ response. Then read your conversation out loud with a partner.**

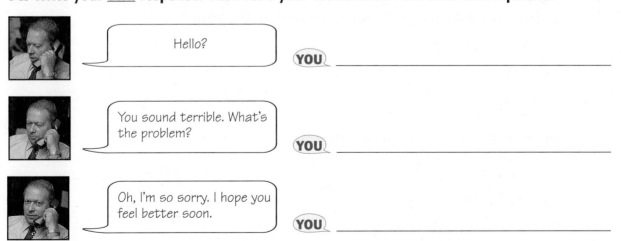

Hello?

YOU _____

You sound terrible. What's the problem?

YOU _____

Oh, I'm so sorry. I hope you feel better soon.

YOU _____

**B.** **Discussion. Talk about your health or the health of a family member.**

# Authentic practice 2

## Reading

**A.** Read Mr. Reyes's accident report. Then check ☑ the boxes. What information does the report ask for?

1. ❑ the worker's name
2. ❑ the worker's address
3. ❑ the worker's date of birth
4. ❑ the worker's place of birth
5. ❑ the worker's phone number
6. ❑ the doctor's name

## Totally Cool Air Conditioners

### ——— Accident Report ———

Employee: _____ *Reyes* _____ *Carlos* _____
          (last name)      (first name)

Date of birth: _____ *11* _____ *3* _____ *67* _____
                    month      day      year

Complete the following section:

Date of accident: _____ *5* _____ *13* _____ *01* _____
                        month      day      year

Place of accident (check one)   ☑ at job   ❑ other

Injury is to (check one)
☑ back or neck          ❑ ankle or foot
❑ hand or wrist         ❑ head
❑ leg                   ❑ other

**B.** **Critical thinking. Look at the two ways to write dates. Then answer the questions. Circle the letter.**

| Words and numbers | Numbers |
|---|---|
| August 2, 1955 | 8/2/55 |
| January 12, 2000 | 1/12/00 |

1. Why do we write August 2, 1955 as 8/2/55?

   **a.** Because August is the eighth month of the year.

   **b.** Because August is the second month of the year.

2. What is the year in 1/12/00?

   **a.** 2000.

   **b.** 2001.

**C.** Write the following dates with numbers.

1. November 3, 1983 _____   2. August 3, 2002 _____

3. June 24, 1986 _____   4. May 13, 2006 _____

**D.** Personalization. Complete the form about yourself. Write the dates in numbers.

Date of birth: _____

Today's date: _____

**Read about Mary Costa's accident. Then complete the emergency room report form.**

On Monday, June 14, 2001, Mary Costa had an accident on her way to work. The accident was at the corner of King Street and North Avenue. She hurt her neck.

**Important information**

- Ms. Costa's address is 84 North Avenue, Madison, New York.

- Her zip code is 10514.

- Her date of birth is September 8, 1944.

- Her phone number is (913) 555-6744.

## ✳ Memorial Hospital

**Emergency Room**                                      **Patient Information**

Patient's name: _____    Date of visit: _____
           first      last or family             month     day     year

Address: _____
          number and street        city        state      zip code

Date of birth: _____    Telephone: _____
        month     day     year          area code     number

## ➤ Do it yourself!

**Pair work. Create a conversation between the receptionist and the patient. Use the picture for ideas. Use your <u>own</u> words.**

## Review

**A.** Vocabulary. **Write the name of each body part on the line.**

1. _____    2. _____    3. _____

4. _____    5. _____    6. _____

**B.** Conversation. **Choose your response. Circle the letter.**

1. "Can you talk?"

    **a.** Not now. I'm sorry.    **b.** This is Ray.

2. "Can I call you back later?"

    **a.** Not now. I'm eating.    **b.** Sure. How about 1:00?

3. "How's Wednesday?"

    **a.** She's fine.    **b.** Fine. See you then.

**C.** Grammar. **Choose words. Write the words on the line.**

1. "Doctor _____ office. How may I help you?"
        Stern / Stern's

2. Ms. Loyola hurt _____ foot in the accident.
                her / their

3. He _____ on the phone right now.
        talks / is talking

4. Juan sometimes _____ to work early.
                is going / goes

**D.** Reading. **Read the report. Then write yes, no, or I don't know.**

1. This is a report of a telephone call.

    _____

2. The car is Sharon Wong's car.

    _____

3. The date of the call is November 3, 2001.

    _____

4. Two people are hurt.

    _____

**CENTER CITY**
**911 Report**

Date: _10/3/01_

Time: _2:56 p.m._

Caller's name: _Sharon Wong_

Place: _corner of Park Street_
_and Main Street_

Problem: _car fire_

> ## ➤ Do it yourself!
>
> **1.** Point. Name things in the picture.
>   *An ambulance*
>
> **2.** Point. Talk about the people.
>   *She hurt her back.*
>
> **3.** Create conversations for the people.
>   *A: There's an accident on Grand Avenue.*
>   *B: Do you need a fire truck?*
>
> **4.** Say more about the picture. Use your <u>own</u> words. Say as much as you can.

Now I can
- ❏ talk about accidents.
- ❏ talk about health.
- ❏ call 911.
- ❏ make an appointment.
- ❏ _____.

# Your money

**Objectives**

- talk about money
- talk about the future
- pay bills
- write checks
- use credit cards

## ▶ Vocabulary

### Picture dictionary

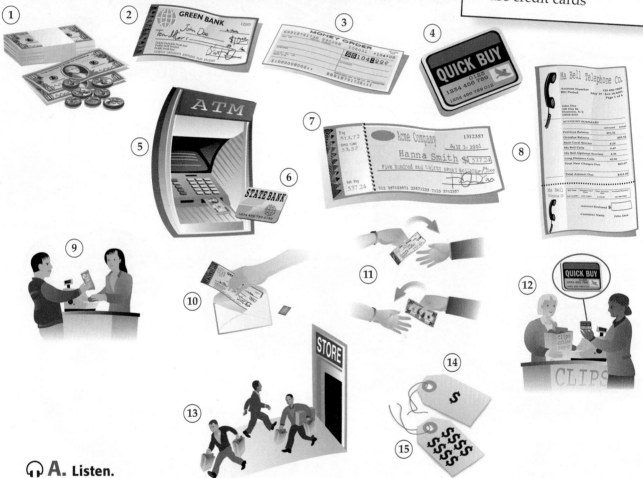

🎧 **A.** Listen.

| Money and payment | | Actions | Other words |
|---|---|---|---|
| ① cash | ⑤ an ATM | ⑨ pay | ⑭ cheap |
| ② a check | ⑥ an ATM card | ⑩ pay by mail | ⑮ expensive |
| ③ a money order | ⑦ a paycheck | ⑪ cash a check | |
| ④ a credit card | ⑧ a bill | ⑫ charge | |
| | | ⑬ go shopping | |

🎧 **B.** Listen again and repeat.

**C.** Listen to the conversations. Look at the pictures. Then listen again and match. Write the letter of the picture on the line.

a.            b.            c.            d.

1. _____    2. _____    3. _____    4. _____

**D.** Complete the sentences. Write the words on the line.

1. Let's _____ our paychecks at the bank. Then we can go shopping.

2. I need to go to the post office to buy a _____. I want to send some money to my father in Mexico.

3. I like to talk on the telephone, but I don't like to pay the _____!

4. The store wants $50 for that book? That's too _____.

➤ Do it yourself!

**A.** Complete the chart.

| Coins | | Bills | |
|---|---|---|---|
| a penny | $ .01 | | $ 1.00 |
| a nickel | $_____ | | $_____ |
| a dime | $_____ | | $_____ |
| a quarter | $_____ | | $_____ |

**B.** Collaborative activity. Complete the chart.

| Amount | Possible combinations |
|---|---|
| $1.00 | 4 quarters, 10 dimes, 5 dimes and 2 quarters, 100 pennies |
| $2.50 | |
| $34.99 | |

**C.** Discussion. Discuss your combinations with the class.

### Model 1    Ask for change.

🎧 **A.** Listen and read.

A: Do you have change for five dollars?
B: Let me check. Yes, I do. Here you go.
A: Thanks.

🎧 **B.** Listen again and repeat.

**C.** Pair work. Now answer <u>Yes, I do</u> or <u>No, I'm sorry. I don't</u>. Use the pictures.

A: Do you have change for _____?
B: Let me check. _____.
A: _____.

### Model 2    Ask for a price.

🎧 **A.** Listen and read.

A: Excuse me. How much is this lawn mower?
B: $300.
A: That's a lot. I'll have to think about it.

🎧 **Problems with prices**
a lot
too expensive
not cheap

🎧 **B.** Listen again and repeat.

**C.** Pair work. Now use the pictures or your <u>own</u> words.

A: Excuse me. How much is this _____?
B: _____.
A: That's _____. I'll have to think about it.

🎧 **A. Listen and read.**

    **A:** How much is this TV?
    **B:** Only $85.99. It's on sale.
    **A:** Great. I'll take it.
    **B:** Will that be cash or charge?
    **A:** Cash.

🎧 **B. Listen again and repeat.**

**C. Pair work. Now use the pictures and your <u>own</u> prices.**

🎧 **How to say it**
- "Eighty-five ninety-nine"
  or
- "Eighty-five dollars and ninety-nine cents"

    **A:** How much is this _____?
    **B:** Only _____. It's on sale.
    **A:** Great. I'll take it.
    **B:** Will that be cash or charge?
    **A:** _____.

# ➤ Do it yourself!

**Pair work. Create a conversation from the picture. Use your <u>own</u> prices.**

## The future

| Tomorrow | I'm you're he's she's we're they're | going to buy a car. |

What **are you going to do** tomorrow?
Who's **going to cash** this check today?

**A.** **Complete the sentences with a form of <u>be going to</u> and the verb.**

1. I'm going to charge these clothes with my Quick Buy credit card.
   <sub>charge</sub>

2. I_____ my paycheck, and then I'm going to go shopping.
   <sub>cash</sub>

3. Next month we_____ new telephones.
   <sub>install</sub>

4. Who_____ all these bills?
   <sub>pay</sub>

5. Why_____ you _____ a car?
   <sub>buy</sub>

**B.** **Pair work. Ask your partner questions about the future. Use <u>be going to</u>.**

1. What are you going to do today?
2. What are you going to do next year?

**Now tell the class about your partner.**

Next year Miriam is going to go to Mexico.

## <u>Whose</u> and review of question words

| Whose | |
|---|---|
| **Whose** check is this? | It's Carla's check. |
| **Whose** shoes are these? | They're my shoes. |

**C.** **Complete the conversations with question words.**

1. **A:** _____ car is in the parking lot?

   **B:** Bill's.

2. **A:** _____ are you going to do at the bank?

   **B:** I'm going to ask for change for a twenty-dollar bill.

3. **A:** _____ are you going to be ready?

   **B:** I don't know. I'm really busy right now.

4. **A:** _____ can't you charge this jacket?

   **B:** Because I don't have a credit card.

**D.** **Form teams. Write questions for each answer in the box. Each question receives 1 point. You have five minutes.**

| Answers | | |
| --- | --- | --- |
| ~~Fourteen.~~ | She's my daughter. | Next year. |
| Brazil. | $2.50, I think. | A large salad. |
| Because they're on sale. | I don't know. | The supply room. |

A: How many bills do you have to pay?
B: Fourteen.

## ➤ Do it yourself!

**A.** **Pair work. Point. Ask questions about the future.**

Is she going to return the jacket?

**B.** **Personalization. Talk to your partner about shopping.**

I'm going to buy shoes tomorrow.

**With words you know, YOU can talk to this cashier.**

**A. Listen and read.**

**Cashier:** That'll be $23.68, including the tax. Will that be cash or charge?

**YOU** *What about a check?*

**Cashier:** Sure. Is it from a local bank?

**YOU** *Excuse me?*

**Cashier:** Where is the check from? What bank?

**YOU** *Oh. It's from the First State Bank. On Clinton Avenue.*

**Cashier:** That's fine. I'll need to see some kind of I.D.

**YOU** *Is a driver's license OK?*

**Cashier:** Yes, that's great. Go ahead and write the check.

**YOU** *Here you go.*

**Cashier:** Thank you. And have a nice day.

**B. Listen to the cashier. Read your part.**

**C. Listen and read. Choose your response. Circle the letter.**

1. "Cash or charge?"

   **a.** Is a check OK?          **b.** Yes.

2. "Do you have I.D.?"

   **a.** I'll take it.          **b.** Let me check. . . . Yes, here you go.

3. "That'll be $200."

   **a.** No problem.          **b.** Do you have change?

**I.D.**

NEW YORK STATE
DRIVER'S LICENSE

a driver's license

GREEN ONION SHOPPER'S CARD
The store with more.
TERRY M. DENZOLIS
40-227-003466      03/19

a check-cashing card

**D. Listen. Choose your response. Circle the letter.**

1. **a.** It's next to the parking lot.     **b.** Yes, it is.

2. **a.** Sure. Here you go.          **b.** Where are you going?

3. **a.** Thanks. Bye.          **b.** It's on sale.

🎧 **A. Listen to the conversation. Then read the sentences. Write <u>yes</u> or <u>no</u>.**

1. The two people talking are a father and a daughter. _____

2. The man pays cash. _____

🎧 **B. Read the questions and answers. Then listen again to answer each question. Circle the letter.**

1. Who is paying the bill?

   **a.** Janet Klein.                    **b.** Janet Klein's father.

2. Where are the people who are talking?

   **a.** In an office in Korea.          **b.** In an office in the United States.

3. Whose bill is it?

   **a.** Janet Klein's.                  **b.** Mr. Klein's.

4. How much is the bill?

   **a.** $50.                            **b.** $45.88.

5. Why does the man want quarters?

   **a.** He's going to pay the bill.     **b.** He's going to need quarters in the parking lot.

---

## ➤ Do it yourself!

**A. Write your <u>own</u> response. Then read your conversation out loud with a partner.**

Is that check from a local bank?

**YOU** _____

Now I'll have to see some form of I.D.

**YOU** _____

Great. Thank you very much. Have a nice day.

**YOU** _____

**B. Discussion. Talk about your I.D. or about bills you have to pay.**

## Reading

**A.** Look at the bill for newspaper delivery. Then check ☑ the information you can find on the bill.

The Journal Gazette

P.O. Box 2274, Elk City, CA 94129-2267

| CUSTOMER SERVICE NUMBER |
| :---: |
| 1-800-555-1010 |

| ACCOUNT NUMBER |
| :---: |
| WT4265427 |

LARRY WILSON
4645 NORTH MAIN
NEWBERG, CA    94104

| DELIVERY PERIOD | PAY BY | AMOUNT DUE |
| :---: | :---: | :---: |
| 3/22/02 to 6/21/02 | 3/4/02 | $55.25 |

1. ☐ the name of the newspaper
2. ☐ the amount the customer has to pay
3. ☐ the customer's telephone number
4. ☐ the newspaper's address
5. ☐ the customer's address
6. ☐ the date payment is due

**B.** Look at Larry Wilson's check. Circle and number these things:

1. the delivery dates
2. the amount of money in numbers
3. the amount of money in words
4. the date of the check

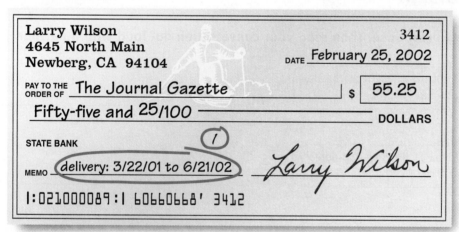

Larry Wilson
4645 North Main
Newberg, CA  94104

3412

DATE February 25, 2002

PAY TO THE ORDER OF   The Journal Gazette      $ 55.25

Fifty-five and 25/100 —————————— DOLLARS

STATE BANK

MEMO  delivery: 3/22/01 to 6/21/02      Larry Wilson

⑴

l:021000089:l b0bb0bb8' 3412

**C.** Critical thinking. Check ☑ the answer.

Mr. Wilson's payment is _____.

☐ early      ☐ on time      ☐ late

**Look at the bill and receipt. Then complete the checks.**

### Southern Phone

CLARA MOLINA
76 SOUTH PLACE
NEW BEACH, FL 32168

| BILL DATE | PAYMENT DUE DATE | AMOUNT DUE |
|---|---|---|
| JUNE 6, 2003 | JUNE 25, 2003 | $90.00 |

---

Clara Molina                                    257
76 South Place
New Beach, FL 32168                 DATE _____

PAY TO THE
ORDER OF _____ $ _____

_____ DOLLARS

MEMO ___ phone bill ___   *Clara Molina*

7:02103009:1 800668' 257          **STATE BANK** ⊕

---

### The Food Basket
August 16, 2003

| | |
|---|---|
| Cheese | 4.59 |
| Eggs | 1.89 |
| Onions | 0.99 |
| Chicken soup | 0.79 |
| Meat | 7.54 |
| Subtotal | 15.80 |
| Tax | 0.00 |
| Amount due | $15.80 |

---

Ivan Dumova                                     152
205 West 95th Street
New York, NY 10025                  DATE _____

PAY TO THE
ORDER OF _____ $ _____

_____ DOLLARS

**NY Bank**
2560 BROADWAY AT 96TH STREET
NEW YORK, NY 10025

MEMO ___ food ___

6:420220089:1 80600668' 152

---

## ➤ Do it yourself!    A plan-ahead project

**Discussion. Bring a bill to class. Compare your bills. Use the pictures for ideas.**

What kind of bill is it?

Can you pay the bill with a check?

How are you going to pay the bill?

# Review

**A. Vocabulary. Choose words. Write the words on the line.**

1.  Is that cash, check, or _____?
    charge / mail

2.  He's going to _____ his paycheck at the bank.
    charge / cash

3.  I'm going to get some money from the _____.
    ATM / bill

4.  I have a lot of _____ to pay this month.
    cash / bills

**B. Conversation. Choose <u>your</u> response. Circle the letter.**

1.  "Do you have change for a dollar?"

    **a.** I'll have to think about it.          **b.** Yes, I do. Are four quarters OK?

2.  "Will that be cash or charge?"

    **a.** It's my paycheck.          **b.** Is a check OK?

3.  "I'll take it."

    **a.** Good. Will that be cash or charge?   **b.** I'll have to check.

**C. Grammar. Complete each sentence with a form of <u>be going to</u> and the verb.**

1.  Tomorrow I_'m going to go shopping_ for new shoes.
    go shopping

2.  They _____ a check to the telephone company.
    write

3.  When _____ you _____ your paycheck?
    cash

4.  How much _____ they _____ for that car?
    pay

**D. Writing. Write a check to pay this bill.**

| Food City | |
|---|---|
| Bread | 1.00 |
| Paper towels | 3.00 |
| Chicken | 9.31 |
| Subtotal | $13.31 |
| Tax | $0.34 |
| Amount due | $13.65 |

| | 304 |
|---|---|
| DATE _____ | |
| PAY TO THE ORDER OF _____ | $ [    ] |
| _____ DOLLARS | |

**Main Bank**
228 Front St.
Plano, TX 75082

MEMO _____      _____

⑈:041000689⑈1  60660668' 304

**➤ Do it yourself!**

**1.** Point. Talk about the people.

*He likes the red tie.*

**2.** Point. Ask your partner about the future.

*Is she going to buy the suit?*

**3.** Create conversations for the people.

*A: Excuse me. How much is this tie?*
*B: $7.99.*

**4.** Say more about the picture. Use your <u>own</u> words. Say as much as you can.

Monday
**6**
NOVEMBER

Now I can
❏ talk about money.
❏ talk about the future.
❏ pay bills.
❏ write checks.
❏ use credit cards.

❏ _____.

Unit 9    119

# Your career

## Vocabulary

### Picture dictionary

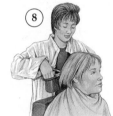

## A. Listen.

**Occupations and skills**

1. a truck driver — drives a truck
2. a nurse's aide — helps nurses
3. a plumber — fixes toilets and sinks
4. a painter — paints houses
5. a telephone technician — installs telephones
6. a dishwasher — washes dishes

**Occupations and skills**

7. a cashier — uses a cash register
8. a hairdresser — cuts hair
9. a receptionist — greets visitors
10. a salesperson — sells
11. a child care worker — takes care of children
12. a dental assistant — helps dentists

### Getting a job

13. a job application     14. an interview

## B. Listen again and repeat.

**How to say it**

a child     children

120     Unit 10

**C.** Listen to the speakers. Circle the letter of the occupations.

1. **a.** a receptionist       **b.** a telephone technician
2. **a.** a plumber            **b.** a child care worker
3. **a.** a nurse's aide       **b.** a dishwasher
4. **a.** a painter            **b.** a hairdresser

**D.** Choose words. Write the words on the line.

1. Your _____ with Mr. Smith is at 11:00. Please be on time.
   interview / application

2. In order to apply for a job here, you need to fill out this job _____.
   application / interview

## ➤ Do it yourself!

**A.** Complete the chart. Then add your <u>own</u> skill and occupation. Or use the pictures.

| Skills | Occupations |
|--------|-------------|
| drive | *a truck driver, a bus driver* |
| wash dishes | |
| use a cash register | |
| | |

a student, a teacher

a doctor, a nurse

a writer

a letter carrier

a sanitation worker

a paramedic

a firefighter

**B.** Pair work. What skill and occupation did <u>you</u> add? Tell your partner.

### Model 1    Talk about skills and experience.

**A.** Listen and read.

> **A:** I'm looking for a job.
> **B:** Good. What skills do you have?
> **A:** Well, I can fix buses and trucks.
> **B:** What was your last job?
> **A:** I was a mechanic.
> **B:** Do you want to fill out an application?
> **A:** Yes, thanks.

**B.** Listen again and repeat.

**C.** Pair work. **Use the information in the box. Then talk about <u>your</u> skills.**

> **A:** I'm looking for a job.
> **B:** _____. What skills do you have?
> **A:** Well, I can _____.
> **B:** What was your last job?
> **A:** I was _____.
> **B:** Do you want to fill out an application?
> **A:** _____.

| Skills | Jobs |
| --- | --- |
| drive a bus | a bus driver |
| fix sinks | a plumber |
| wash dishes | a dishwasher |
| install telephones | a telephone technician |

### Model 2    Describe your personal qualities.

**A.** Listen and read.

> **A:** Do you have any experience?
> **B:** Well, not really. But I'm a good worker, and I learn fast.
> **A:** That's great. Can you come for an interview tomorrow?
> **B:** Sure.

**B.** Listen again and repeat.

**C.** Pair work. **Now use your <u>own</u> words.**

**A:** Do you have any experience?

**B:** Well, not really. But I'm a good worker, and I learn fast.

**A:** _____. Can you come for an interview _____?

**B:** _____.

## Model 3   Ask about the past.

🎧 **A.** **Listen and read.**

**A:** So, Claudia, what did you do in Mexico?

**B:** Oh, me? I was a nurse.

**A:** A nurse! That's interesting! How long did you do that?

**B:** For four years. What about you? What did you do?

**A:** In China I was a homemaker.

🎧 **B.** **Listen again and repeat.**

**C.** Pair work. **Now talk about your <u>own</u> life.**

**A:** So, _____, what did you do in _____?

**B:** Oh, me? I was _____.

**A:** _____! That's interesting! How long did you do that?

**B:** _____. What about you? What did you do?

**A:** In _____ I was _____.

🎧 **Periods of time**

For four years.
From 1998 to 2001.

## ➤ Do it yourself!

**A.** Pair work. **Create a job interview from the picture. Talk about experience and skills. Use your <u>own</u> words.**

**B.** Personalization. **Work with a partner. Talk about your skills and experience. Ask and answer these questions.**

- What skills do you have?

- What did you do in your country?

- How long did you do that?

# Practical grammar

## The past tense of <u>be</u>

Talk about the past with <u>was</u>, <u>were</u>, <u>wasn't</u>, and <u>weren't</u>.

I
He } **was** a nurse for two years.
She

We
You } **were** nurses in China.
They

She **wasn't** at work on Monday. They **weren't** at school.

**A.** Choose words. Write the words on the line.

1. Francisco _____ a cook in his country. He was a restaurant manager.
   weren't / wasn't

2. Carol and Chen _____ receptionists from 1999 to 2000.
   was / were

3. Yong _____ a student in 1998. Now he's a child care worker.
   was / were

4. I _____ a dental assistant for seven years.
   was / were

5. We _____ dishwashers at Bill's Restaurant. We were cashiers.
   were / weren't

6. She _____ a technician. She was a nurse's aide.
   wasn't / weren't

**Questions**

**Were** you a cook in your country?          Yes, I **was**. /No, I **wasn't**.
How long **were** you a receptionist?          For three years.
Who **was** your manager?          Mr. Cortez.

**B.** Choose words. Write the words on the line.

1. Where _____ in 1998?
   they were / were they

2. When _____ a plumber?
   he was / was he

3. Who _____ at the supermarket?
   were / was

4. Why _____ in the hospital?
   you were / were you

5. _____ you at work yesterday?
   Were / Was

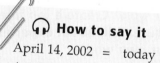

**How to say it**

April 14, 2002 = today
April 13 = yesterday
April 7–13 = last week
March = last month
2001 = last year

A: What **did** you **do** at your last job?

B: I **helped** customers.

A: **Did** you **use** a cash register?

B: Yes, I **did**. But I **didn't use** a computer.

**Regular past forms**

| | |
|---|---|
| help | **helped** |
| wash | **washed** |
| fix | **fixed** |
| install | **installed** |
| use | **used** |
| paint | **painted** |
| greet | **greeted** |

**Irregular past forms**

| | |
|---|---|
| cut | **cut** |
| drive | **drove** |
| sell | **sold** |
| take | **took** |

See page 140 for more irregular past forms.

**C.** **Write the simple past tense on the line.**

1. Last year we _____ the kitchen green.
   <br>paint

2. From 1997 to 1998, Carl _____ plumbing supplies, but now he's a plumber.
   <br>sell

3. I _____ at Broadway Hair Design for six months. First I was the
   <br>work

   receptionist, and then I _____ hair.
   <br>cut

4. Who _____ this microwave oven? Joe? He didn't clean the door!
   <br>use

5. Elena _____ the dishes in the kitchen. The sink was out of order.
   <br>not wash

## ➤ Do it yourself!

**A.** **Pair work. Ask and answer questions about the picture.**

A: What was his last job?

B: He was a cashier.

**B.** **Personalization. Ask your partner about himself or herself.**

A: What did you do at your last job?

B: I painted houses.

**With words you know, YOU can talk to this dentist.**

🎧 **A. Listen and read.**

**Dentist:** So, you're interested in the dental assistant opening at Family Dental Care.

**YOU** Yes, I am.

**Dentist:** That's great. We need several dental assistants right now. What kind of experience do you have?

**YOU** Well, in Korea I was a dental assistant in a small dental office. Two dentists worked there.

**Dentist:** Do you have experience as a dental assistant in this country?

**YOU** Well, not really. But I'm a good worker, Dr. Martins.

**Dentist:** Excellent. When would you be available to start work here at Family Dental Care?

**YOU** In two weeks.

🎧 **B. Listen to the dentist. Read your part.**

🎧 **C. Listen and read. Choose your response. Circle the letter.**

1. "I understand that you're interested in a job at Happy Holiday Hotels."

   **a.** Yes. I want to be an assistant manager.   **b.** That's interesting.

2. "What kind of experience do you have working in hotels?"

   **a.** I was a manager of a small hotel for three years.   **b.** I'm a good worker.

3. "When can you start work here?"

   **a.** From Monday to Friday.   **b.** In a week.

## D. Listen. Choose your response. Circle the letter.

1. **a.** Is next Monday OK?     **b.** From 1997 to 1999.

2. **a.** Not yet.     **b.** In 1999.

3. **a.** Yes, I am.     **b.** Let me check.

## Listening comprehension

### A. Listen to the conversation. Then complete the sentences. Circle the letter.

1. Ms. Miglin wants _____.    **a.** a job     **b.** some office supplies

2. Mr. Downs is a _____.    **a.** store manager     **b.** cashier

### B. Read the sentences. Then listen again. Write yes or no.

1. Ms. Miglin wants a job as a cashier. _____

2. Ms. Miglin worked at Golden Office Supplies for six years. _____

3. Ms. Miglin has experience as a salesperson. _____

4. Ms. Miglin worked in the computer sales department. _____

5. Ms. Miglin can start work tomorrow. _____

## ➤ Do it yourself!

### A. Write your own response. Then read your conversation out loud with a partner.

So, you're interested in working at this company.

**YOU** _____

What kind of experience do you have?

**YOU** _____

When can you start working here?

**YOU** _____

### B. Discussion. Talk about an interview or about your last job.

# Authentic practice 2

## Reading

**A.** Read the ads. Answer the questions.

**a**

Company: Brown
Construction Company
Position: Electrician's
assistant
Experience required.
☑ Part-time   ☐ Full-time
Hours: 9:00 to 1:00
For an interview call
555-1000.

**b**  Good Neighbor Direct • 4338 DiPaolo Center, Glenview IL 60025 • (800) 772-2229

**FREE AD**

Position: Housekeeper        | Phone
Part-time
Hours: 7:00 to 12:00         | Phone
No experience required.
Apply at the 100 Garden      | Phone
Street entrance.
Name Northview Hotel Date___ | Phone

**c**

Company: General Hospital
Position: Nurse's aide
☐ Part-time   ☑ Full-time
Hours: 6:00 to 2:00
Experience required.
Apply at 30 River Road.

**d**  Good Neighbor Direct • 4338 DiPaolo Center, Glenview IL 60025 • (800) 772-2229

**FREE AD**

Position: Plumber's helper   | Phone
No experience required.
Driver's license required.   | Phone
Full-time
Hours: 7:00 to 3:30          | Phone
Call 555-1234 for an
interview.
Name Express     Date___     | Phone
Plumbing

**e**

Company: Office of
Dr. Jose Mendoza
Position: Nurse
Experience is required
☐ Part-time   ☑ Full-time
Hours: 10:00 to 5:00
Call 555-2380 for an
interview.

**f**  Good Neighbor Direct • 4338 DiPaolo Center, Glenview IL 60025 • (800) 772-2229

**FREE AD**

Position: Child care worker  | Phone
No experience required.
Part-time                    | Phone
Hours: 3:30 to 6:00
Apply at 215 Bridge Street   | Phone
after 2:30.
Name Child Care Center Date__| Phone

1. How many jobs are full-time? _____

2. How many jobs require experience? _____

🎧 **Full-time and part-time**

**full-time** = 40 hours per week
**part-time** = under 40 hours,
for example, 20 hours per week

**B.** Critical thinking. **These people want jobs.
Where can they apply? Write the letter of the ad.**

Espinoza

1. Right now Rosa Espinoza is a homemaker. She has no job experience,
but she can fix microwaves, lights, sinks, and toilets. She can fix cars
and trucks, too. She has a driver's license. She needs a full-time job.

_____

Romano

2. Lisa Romano works at Best Supermarket every day from 8:00 to 2:00.
She wants a part-time job. She likes to take care of children. She likes
to cook and clean, too. _____

Salem

3. Jamal Salem was a nurse in his country. He can take a full-time or a
part-time job. He has three small children. His wife's job starts at 4:00.
Jamal needs to be home at 3:00 to take care of his children. _____

**128**      Unit 10

**A.** Ana Menendez filled out this job application for a job at the Northview Hotel. Read the application. Answer the questions.

Applicant: _Ana Menendez_     Position: _part-time housekeeper_

| Employer or place | Job | Experience or skills | Dates |
|---|---|---|---|
| Mrs. Joan Crane 12 Ocean Drive Malibu, California | part-time housekeeper | I clean Mrs. Crane's house. | 1/99 to now |
| In Peru I was a homemaker for 19 years. | full-time homemaker | I cooked, cleaned, and took care of my children. | 1980 to 1999 |

1.  What does Ms. Menendez do at her job? _____

2.  What did she do from 1980 to 1999? What skills did she use? _____

    _____

    _____

**B.** Complete the application. Write about yourself.

Applicant: _____     Position: _____

| Employer or place | Job | Experience or skills | Dates |
|---|---|---|---|
|  |  |  |  |
|  |  |  |  |

➤ **Do it yourself!**     A plan-ahead project

**Pair work. Bring in help-wanted ads from a newspaper. Choose a job. Practice your interview.**

- Partner A is an interviewer.
- Partner B is a job applicant.

# Review

### A. Vocabulary. Complete the chart. Write a skill for each occupation.

| Occupation | Skill |
|---|---|
| 1. hairdresser | |
| 2. child care worker | |
| 3. Your occupation: | |

### B. Conversation. Choose <u>your</u> response. Circle the letter.

1. "Do you have any experience?"

   a. Yes. I was a cashier in a clothes store.    b. I'm looking for a job.

2. "That's great! How long did you do that?"

   a. In my country.    b. For three years.

3. "Do you want to fill out an application?"

   a. I can learn fast.    b. Yes, please.

### C. Grammar. Write the past tense form of the verb.

1. Carlos ___*opened*___ the store at 9:00 this morning.
   open

2. At my old job, I _____ customers.
   greet

3. Who _____ your hair? It looks great!
   cut

4. How long _____ you a nurse's aide?
   be

5. I _____ that truck. Robert fixed it.
   not fix

### D. Reading. Read the ad. Then read about Alicia Fernandez. Can Ms. Fernandez apply for the job? Write <u>yes</u> or <u>no</u>.

Alicia Fernandez was a part-time truck driver in Mexico. She worked from 1998 to 1999. Now she's looking for a full-time job. _____

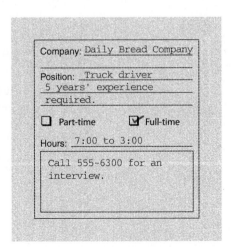

**1.** Point. Talk about occupations and skills.

*He's a bus driver. He can drive a bus.*

**2.** Point. Talk about the people.

*She filled out a job application.*

**3.** Create conversations for the people.

*A: In Mexico I installed telephones.*
*B: Do you have any experience here?*

**4.** Say more about the picture. Use your <u>own</u> words. Say as much as you can.

Now I can
- ☐ talk about my skills and experience.
- ☐ talk about the past.
- ☐ interview for a job.
- ☐ fill out an application.
- ☐ _____ .

# Vocabulary reference lists

This is an alphabetical list of all active vocabulary in *Workplace Plus* 1. The numbers refer to the page on which the word first appears. When a word has two meanings (a <u>can</u> of soup OR I <u>can</u> read), both are in the list.

**A**

a   12
accident   96
across from   27
address   5
always   100
am   16
a.m.   62
ambulance   96
an   12
and   26
ankle   96
any   74
apple   72
application   120
apply   121
appointment   98
are   16
area code   10
arm   96
aspirin   97
at   29
at home   29
at school   29
at work   29
ATM   108
ATM card   108

**B**

backache   96
bag   74
bank   24
bean   72
because   86
between   27
bill   108
black   48
blue   48
book   4
bottle   74
box   74
bread   72
brother   84
brown   48
bus   12

bus driver   12
busy   86
but   15
button   36
buy   72

**C**

call   36
call back   98
can   *n.*   74
can   *v.*   88
car   86
carrot   72
cash   *n.*   108
cash a check   *v.*   108
cash register   36
cashier   12
cent   111
change   110
charge   108
cheap   108
check   *n.*   108
check   *v.*   108
check-cashing card   114
cheese   72
chicken   72
child   120
child care worker   120
chop   81
circle   1
class   4
classmate   4
clean   84
clothes   48
close   36
coffee   72
coffee maker   36
coins   109
cold   96
color   48
come   84
computer   36
containers   74
conversation   2
cook   12
corner   99

copier   36
credit card   114
cup   81
customer   48
cut   120

**D**

date   64
daughter   84
day   60
dental assistant   120
dentist   120
dime   109
directions   36
dish   120
dishwasher   120
do   *aux.*   50
do   *v.*   86
doctor   96
dollar   110
door   36
down the hall   26
dress   48
drink   72
drive   84
driver   12
driver's license   114

**E**

early   66
eat   72
egg   72
electrician   12
emergency room   96
end   62
engineer   12
entrance   24
exchange   56
exit   24
expensive   108
experience   120

**F**

fast   122
father   84

This is a unit-by-unit list of all the social language from the practical conversations in *Workplace Plus* 1.

## Welcome to *Workplace Plus*

Hello.
I'm Carmen.
Hi.
Nice to meet you.
Nice to meet you too.
Mary, this is John. John, this is Mary.
Is that M-A-R-Y? (for clarification)
What's your name, please?
Is that your first name?
And what's your last name?
Thank you.
What's your address?
Is that 30 or 13? (for clarification)
Thanks.
You're welcome.
What's your phone number?
And your area code?

## Unit 1

Are you Ken Wang?
Yes, I am./No, I'm not.
Oh, hi.
Good to meet you.
Where are you from?
What about you?
What do you do?
And you?
Oh, I'm sorry. (to express sympathy)
Well, good luck!

## Unit 2

Excuse me? (to ask for repetition)
Excuse me. (to initiate a conversation)
I'm looking for the _____.
The _____? (to ask for clarification)

## Unit 3

Oh, no! (to express dismay)
What's wrong?
Let's _____ (as in How do I _____?) (for suggestions)
Good idea.
OK. No problem. (to agree to a command)
How do I _____? (to ask for directions)
OK. (to express comprehension)
I don't know.

## Unit 4

Sure. (to express willingness)
OK. (to express willingness)
This way, please.
I'm sorry. (to apologize)
May I help you?
Yes, please.
Yes, I think so.

## Unit 5

What time is it?
Uh-oh. (to express dismay)
Bye.
See you later.
I'm not sure.
_____, I think. (to express an opinion)
That's great! (to express enthusiasm)

## Unit 6

What's up?
Not much.
Anything else?
No, that's all.
Not me.
What about milk?
Me too!
We're out of _____.

## Unit 7

Not yet.
OK. (to express permission)
Well, _____. (to introduce a thought)

## Unit 8

Hello? (to answer the telephone)
This is Bill. (telephone identification)
Can you talk?
Can I call you back?
Sure. No problem. (to agree to a request)
Talk to you later.
How can I help you? (formal telephone answering)
How about 10:30? (to agree to a time)
That's fine. (to agree to a date)
See you then.
Feel better!
Thanks a lot.
It's on its way.

## Unit 9

Do you have change for twenty dollars?
Let me check.
Here you go.
How much is this _____? (to ask for a price)
That's a lot. (to respond to a price)
I'll have to think about it.
Only $85. (to suggest that a price is low)
It's on sale.
I'll take it. (to agree to buy)
Will that be cash or charge?

## Unit 10

I'm looking for a job.
What was your last job?
Do you want to fill out an application?
Do you have any experience?
Well, not really.
So, _____? (to introduce a question)
Oh, me?
That's interesting!

## Irregular verbs

The following verbs from *Workplace Plus* 1 have irregular past-tense forms.

| Verb | Past-tense form |
|------|-----------------|
| be | was / were |
| buy | bought |
| can | could |
| come | came |
| cut | cut |
| do | did |
| drink | drank |
| drive | drove |
| eat | ate |
| go | went |
| have | had |
| hurt | hurt |
| know | knew |
| make | made |
| meet | met |
| pay | paid |
| read | read |
| sell | sold |
| take | took |
| think | thought |
| write | wrote |

## Days

| | |
|--|--|
| Monday | Friday |
| Tuesday | Saturday |
| Wednesday | Sunday |
| Thursday | |

## Months

| | |
|--|--|
| January | July |
| February | August |
| March | September |
| April | October |
| May | November |
| June | December |

## Numbers

### Cardinal numbers

| | | | |
|--|--|--|--|
| 1 | one | 16 | sixteen |
| 2 | two | 17 | seventeen |
| 3 | three | 18 | eighteen |
| 4 | four | 19 | nineteen |
| 5 | five | 20 | twenty |
| 6 | six | 21 | twenty-one |
| 7 | seven | 30 | thirty |
| 8 | eight | 40 | forty |
| 9 | nine | 50 | fifty |
| 10 | ten | 60 | sixty |
| 11 | eleven | 70 | seventy |
| 12 | twelve | 80 | eighty |
| 13 | thirteen | 90 | ninety |
| 14 | fourteen | 100 | one hundred |
| 15 | fifteen | 200 | two hundred |

| | |
|--|--|
| 1,000 | one thousand |
| 1,000,000 | one million |
| 1,000,000,000 | one billion |

### Ordinal numbers

| | |
|--|--|
| first | seventeenth |
| second | eighteenth |
| third | nineteenth |
| fourth | twentieth |
| fifth | twenty-first |
| sixth | twenty-second |
| seventh | thirtieth |
| eighth | thirty-first |
| ninth | fortieth |
| tenth | fiftieth |
| eleventh | sixtieth |
| twelfth | seventieth |
| thirteenth | eightieth |
| fourteenth | ninetieth |
| fifteenth | hundredth |
| sixteenth | thousandth |

Following are lists of additional words to expand the vocabulary of each unit. These optional word lists contain a maximum of 20 words.

## Unit 1

### More countries and nationalities

These are the 20 largest recent immigrant groups.

If your country or nationality isn't here, write it on the lines at the bottom of the list.

| | |
|---|---|
| China | Chinese |
| Colombia | Colombian |
| Cuba | Cuban |
| Dominican Republic | Dominican |
| El Salvador | Salvadoran |
| Greece | Greek |
| Guatemala | Guatemalan |
| Haiti | Haitian |
| India | Indian |
| Iran | Iranian |
| Jamaica | Jamaican |
| Korea | Korean |
| Mexico | Mexican |
| Philippines | Filipino |
| Poland | Polish |
| Portugal | Portuguese |
| Russia | Russian |
| Taiwan | Taiwanese |
| Ukraine | Ukrainian |
| Vietnam | Vietnamese |

_____          _____
<u>My</u> country              <u>My</u> nationality

Where do your classmates come from? List any other countries and nationalities.

_____          _____

_____          _____

_____          _____

## Unit 2

### More places

an adult school
a college
a daycare center
a high school

a barber shop
a beauty shop

a movie theater
a shopping mall

a church
a mosque
a synagogue
a temple

an auto repair shop
a bus station
a factory
a garage
a laundromat
a library
a train station
a warehouse

## Unit 3

### More equipment and machines

a cassette player
a CD player
a conveyor
a drill
a dryer
a forklift
a hammer
an iron
a jackhammer
a lathe
a power saw
a radio
a saw
a screwdriver

a sewing machine
a shovel
a stove
a TV
a washing machine

## Unit 4

### More stores

an auto parts store
a bookstore
a bakery
a candy store
a car dealership
a computer store
a convenience store
a department store
a discount store
a drugstore
an electronics store
a florist
a grocery store
a hardware store
an office supply store
a paint store
a plumbing supply store
a secondhand store
a shoe store
a video store

## Unit 5

### More time telling

three ten
ten after three
ten after
ten past three
ten past

three fifteen
a quarter after three
a quarter after
a quarter past three
a quarter past

three thirty
half past three
half past

three forty-five
a quarter to four
a quarter to
a quarter of four
a quarter of

## Unit 6

### More foods

butter
yogurt

a banana
an orange
a peach
a pear

broccoli
a pea
a potato

a pita
a tortilla

a cake
a cookie
a pie

ketchup
mustard
oil
pepper
salt
vinegar

## Unit 7
### More family members

a baby
an uncle
an aunt
a nephew
a niece
a cousin

a grandfather
a grandmother
a grandson
a granddaughter

a father-in-law
a mother-in-law
a son-in-law
a daughter-in-law
a brother-in-law
a sister-in-law

a stepfather
a stepmother
a stepson
a stepdaughter
a stepbrother
a stepsister

## Unit 8
### More body parts

a chest
an elbow
a finger
a fingernail
hair
a knee
a shoulder
a toe
a waist

a cheek
an ear
an eye
a face
a mouth
a nose
a tongue
a tooth

## Unit 9
### More documents

a birth certificate
a business card
a debit card
a fare card
a green card
an insurance card
a library card
a passport
a state I.D. card
a student I.D. card
a traveler's check
a visa
a work authorization permit

## Unit 10
### More occupations

a barber
a beautician
a busboy
a carpenter
a construction worker
a doorman
a file clerk
a florist
a gardener
a janitor
a locksmith
an optician
an orderly
a seamstress
a security guard
a stock clerk
a tailor
a teller
a travel agent
a waiter / waitress

# My address book

Name _____     Telephone (_____)_____

Address _____


Name _____     Telephone (_____)_____

Address _____


Name _____     Telephone (_____)_____

Address _____


Name _____     Telephone (_____)_____

Address _____


Name _____     Telephone (_____)_____

Address _____


Name _____     Telephone (_____)_____

Address _____

# My address book

Name _____     Telephone (_____)_____

Address _____


Name _____     Telephone (_____)_____

Address _____


Name _____     Telephone (_____)_____

Address _____


Name _____     Telephone (_____)_____

Address _____


Name _____     Telephone (_____)_____

Address _____


Name _____     Telephone (_____)_____

Address _____

## My address book

Name _____     Telephone (_____)_____

Address _____


Name _____     Telephone (_____)_____

Address _____


Name _____     Telephone (_____)_____

Address _____


Name _____     Telephone (_____)_____

Address _____


Name _____     Telephone (_____)_____

Address _____


Name _____     Telephone (_____)_____

Address _____

# Grammar Booster

## UNIT 1

### 1. The verb be: statements with singular subjects

| AFFIRMATIVE | | |
|---|---|---|
| Subject | be | |
| I | am | |
| You | are | |
| He | | a student. |
| She | is | |
| Ken | | |
| It | is | a car. |

| NEGATIVE | | | |
|---|---|---|---|
| Subject | be | not | |
| I | am | | |
| You | are | | |
| He | | not | a plumber. |
| She | is | | |
| Ken | | | |
| It | is | not | a bus. |

**A.** Complete the sentences. Use **I**, **You**, **He**, **She**, or **It**.

1. _You_ are a student.

2. _____ is a plumber.

3. _____ am not an electrician.

4. _____ are not my partner.

5. _____ is a cashier.

6. _____ is a car.

### 2. Contractions with the verb be

| Affirmative contractions | Negative contractions |
|---|---|
| I + am = I'm | I + am not = I'm not |
| you + are = you're | you + are not = you're not or you aren't |
| he + is + he's | he + is not = he's not or he isn't |
| she + is = she's | she + is not = she's not or she isn't |
| it + is = it's | it + is not = it's not or it isn't |

Things to remember

you + are + not = { you're not / you aren't

he + is + not = { he's not / he isn't

**B.** **Write the sentences. Use contractions for the underlined words.**

1. <u>He is</u> a teacher.    *He's a teacher.*

2. <u>You are</u> a student.    _____

3. <u>She is</u> from China.    _____

4. <u>I am</u> your partner.    _____

5. <u>It is</u> a picture.    _____

6. He <u>is not</u> in class.    _____

7. You <u>are not</u> a manager.    _____

8. <u>I am</u> not from California.    _____

**C.** **Look at the information in the chart. Write one negative sentence and one affirmative sentence for each person. Use contractions.**

| Person | Occupation |
| --- | --- |
| Ken | a plumber |
| Luis | a cook |
| I | a student |

| Person | Occupation |
| --- | --- |
| you | a teacher |
| Maria | a homemaker |
| Emily | a housekeeper |

1. Ken / a manager    *Ken isn't a manager. He's a plumber.*

2. Luis / a plumber    _____

3. I / a teacher    _____

4. You / a mechanic    _____

5. Marie / a cashier    _____

6. Emily / a bus driver    _____

## 3. The verb be: <u>yes</u> / <u>no</u> questions and short answers

| Be | Subject | |
| --- | --- | --- |
| **Am** | I | your partner? |
| **Are** | you | a manager? |
| **Is** | he | |
| | she | from Greece? |
| | it | |

| Short answers | |
| --- | --- |
| Yes, you are. | No, you aren't. |
| Yes, I am. | No, I'm not. |
| Yes, he is. | No, he isn't. |
| Yes, she is. | No, she isn't. |
| Yes, it is. | No, it isn't. |

**D.** Put the words in order. Write the <u>yes</u> / <u>no</u> questions. Complete the answers.

1. **A:** _Are you a cashier_____?
   you / a cashier / Are

   **B:** No, I _'m not_____.

2. **A:** _____?
   Marta / Is / from Cuba

   **B:** Yes, she _____.

3. **A:** _____?
   a mechanic / he / Is

   **B:** No, he _____.

4. **A:** _____?
   my partner / you / Are

   **B:** Yes, I _____.

5. **A:** _____?
   she / from Russia / Is

   **B:** No, she _____.

6. **A:** _____?
   it / Is / your bus

   **B:** No, it _____.

## 4. <u>A</u> and <u>an</u>

| <u>a</u> | <u>an</u> |
|---|---|
| He is **a** <u>c</u>ook. | He is **an** <u>e</u>lectrician. |
| Is she **a** <u>h</u>ousekeeper? | I am **an** <u>e</u>ngineer. |

**E.** Complete the conversations with a form of <u>be</u> and <u>a</u> or <u>an</u>.

1. **A:** _Is he a_____ manager?

   **B:** _No, he isn't.  He's a teacher._____

2. **A:** _____ electrician?

   **B:** _____

3. **A:** _____ mechanic?

   **B:** _____

4. **A:** _____ cashier?

   **B:** _____

# UNIT 2

## 1. The verb <u>be</u>: statements with plural subjects

| Subject | <u>be</u> | |
|---------|-----------|---|
| We | | |
| You | **are** | here. |
| They | | |

| Subject | <u>be</u> | <u>not</u> | |
|---------|-----------|------------|---|
| We | | | |
| You | **are** | **not** | at work. |
| They | | | |

| Affirmative contractions | Negative contractions |
|--------------------------|-----------------------|
| we + are = we**'re** | we + are not = we**'re not** or we **aren't** |
| you + are = you**'re** | you + are not = you**'re not** or you **aren't** |
| they + are + they**'re** | they + are = they**'re not** or they **aren't** |

**A.** **Complete the sentences. Use contractions.**

1. You and I are partners. <u>We're</u> partners.

2. Jean-Paul and Laurence are not here. _____ at work.

3. You and Jorge are in class. _____ in class.

4. Ivan and I are at school. _____ at school.

5. The teachers are not in Room 5. _____ in Room 3.

6. Luisa and Maria are from Mexico. _____ from Mexico.

**B.** **Complete the sentences. Use contractions.**

1. Grace and Sandra ___<u>aren't</u>___ at school.
   <sub>not</sub>

2. We _____ in Room 10. We're in Room 11.
   <sub>not</sub>

3. You _____ on Main Street.
   <sub>not</sub>

4. They _____ in the office.
   <sub>not</sub>

5. Ricky and I _____ in English class.
   <sub>not</sub>

6. You and Tracy _____ in Meeting Room B.
   <sub>not</sub>

## 2. The verb <u>be</u>: <u>yes</u> / <u>no</u> questions and short answers

| Be | Subject | |
|---|---|---|
| | we | |
| Are | you | on Hill Street? |
| | they | |

| Short answers | | | | |
|---|---|---|---|---|
| | you **are**. | | you **aren't**. |
| Yes, | we **are**. | No, | we **aren't**. |
| | they **are**. | | they **aren't**. |

**C.** Complete the conversations. Write the words on the line.

1. **A:** Igor and Yuri, are you from Russia?

   **B:** Yes, ____we are____.

2. **A:** Are Ms. Martinez and Mr. Chen here today?

   **B:** Yes, _____.

3. **A:** Are Alberto and Hector here?

   **B:** No, _____.

4. **A:** _____ partners?

   **B:** Yes, we are.

5. **A:** _____ partners?

   **B:** No, they're not.

6. **A:** Are you and Nadia from Russia?

   **B:** No, _____.

## 3. The verb <u>be</u>: information questions

| Question word | <u>be</u> | Subject |
|---|---|---|
| **What** | is | your address? |
| **Where** | is | Mrs. Gray? |
| **Where** | are | the exits? |
| **Who** | is | she? |
| **Who** | are | you? |
| | | they? |

| Answers |
|---|
| It's 11 Park Street. |
| She's in the office. |
| They're down the hall. |
| She's the manager. |
| I'm a new student. |
| They're students. |

| Contractions |
|---|
| what + is = **what's** |
| where + is = **where's** |
| who + is = **who's** |

**D.** Complete the questions. Write the words from the box.

| What | What's | ~~Where~~ | Where's | Who | Who's |
|---|---|---|---|---|---|

1. _Where_ are the restrooms?     They're down the hall, on the left.

2. _____ your partner?     Maria.

3. _____ next to the hospital?     A parking lot.

4. _____ he from?     Mexico City.

5. _____ is your occupation?     I'm a mechanic.

6. _____ are they?     They're teachers.

**E.** Complete the conversations. Ask questions with <u>Where</u>. Give directions. Use <u>on</u>, <u>next to</u>, <u>across from</u>, or <u>between . . . and</u>.

1.  **A:** <u>Where is</u>_____ the bank?

    **B:** It's _____ the post office.  It's _____ the restaurant.

2.  **A:** _____ the hospital?

    **B:** It's _____ the school.  It's _____ the parking lot.

3.  **A:** _____ the restaurant?

    **B:** It's _____ Main Street.  It's _____ the hospital.

4.  **A:** _____ the school?

    **B:** It's _____ the post office _____ the supermarket.

# U N I T   3

## 1. Suggestions with <u>Let's</u>

**A.** Write suggestions with <u>Let's</u>.

1. start / the lawn mower

   <u>Let's start the lawn</u>

   <u>mower.</u>

3. unplug / the coffee maker

   _____

   _____

2. read / the book _____

   _____

   _____

4. press / the button _____

   _____

   _____

## 2. Commands

| | |
|---|---|
| **Start** the computer. | **Don't start** the computer. |
| Please **close** the door. | Please **don't close** the door. |
| **Close** the door, please. | |

**B.** **Look at the pictures. Complete the sentences. Use commands.**

1.  Please ____close____ the door.

2.  _Don't start_ the coffee maker.

3.  _____ the key.

4.  Please _____ the microwave.

5.  _____ 911!

6. _____ the <u>on</u> button, please.

---

# U N I T   4

## 1. The simple present tense: affirmative statements

| Subject | Verb | |
|---|---|---|
| I | | |
| We | **like** | |
| You | **want** | new clothes. |
| They | **need** | |
| Bob and Ann | | |

| Subject | Verb | |
|---|---|---|
| He | **likes** | |
| She | | |
| It | **wants** | new clothes. |
| Jack | **needs** | |

**A.** **Complete the sentences with the correct form of the verb.**

1. John ___wants___ brown shoes.
   want / wants

2. You _____ a uniform.
   need / needs

3. She _____ black dresses.
   like / likes

4. I _____ new blue shoes.
   want / wants

5. They _____ new pants.
   want / wants

6. We _____ that store.
   like / likes

7. Tim and Al _____ suits.
   need / needs

8. Grace and I _____ red skirts.
   like / likes

## 2. Have: statements

| Subject | have | |
|---|---|---|
| I | | |
| We | | |
| You | **have** | books. |
| They | | |
| Bob and Ann | | |

| Subject | has | |
|---|---|---|
| He | | |
| She | | |
| It | **has** | books. |
| Jack | | |

**B.** **Complete each sentence.  Write <u>have</u> or <u>has</u> on the line.**

1. She ___*has*___ a car.

2. I _____ new shoes.

3. They _____ brown uniforms.

4. The customer _____ the receipt.

5. You and I _____ books.

6. That store _____ nice clothes.

7. You _____ the wrong size.

8. He _____ the wrong color shirt.

## 3. The simple present tense:  negative statements

| Subject | do not | Base form of the verb | |
|---|---|---|---|
| I | | like | |
| We | | want | |
| You | **do not** | need | red pants. |
| They | | have | |
| Andrei and Eva | | | |

| Subject | does not | Base form of the verb | |
|---|---|---|---|
| He | | like | |
| She | | want | |
| It | **does not** | need | red pants. |
| Marta | | have | |

**Things to remember**

**Contractions:**
do + not = **don't**
does + not = **doesn't**

Be careful!  Don't use to after
<u>do not</u>, <u>don't</u>, <u>does not</u>, or
<u>doesn't</u>.

We do not want coffee.
NOT ~~We do not to want coffee.~~

**C.** **Complete each sentence with the simple present tense.  Use contractions.**

1. I ___*don't like*___ orange shirts.
   <small>not like</small>

2. We _____ jackets.
   <small>not need</small>

3. You _____ this size.
   <small>not want</small>

4. She _____ that store.
   <small>not like</small>

5. We _____ uniforms.
   <small>not need</small>

6. He _____ old clothes.
   <small>not want</small>

7. Ed and Bill _____ ties.
   <small>not like</small>

8. Max _____ a new suit.
   <small>not need</small>

**D.** Look at the list. Complete the sentences. Write <u>have</u>, <u>has</u>, <u>don't have</u>, or <u>doesn't have</u>.

|  | a suit | shirts | shoes | pants | skirts | a jacket |
|---|---|---|---|---|---|---|
| Carlos | ✓ | ✓ | ✓ | ✓ | | |
| Marisol | | ✓ | ✓ | ✓ | | ✓ |
| Jin | | ✓ | ✓ | | ✓ | |

1. Carlos _____*has*_____ a suit, but he ___*doesn't have*___ a jacket.

2. Marisol and Jin _____ shirts, but they _____ suits.

3. Marisol _____ a jacket, but she _____ skirts.

4. Jin _____ skirts, but she _____ pants.

5. Carlos _____ pants, but he _____ skirts!

## 4. The simple present tense: <u>yes</u> / <u>no</u> questions and short answers

| Do / Does | Subject | Base form of the verb | |
|---|---|---|---|
| Do | I | | |
| | we | | |
| | you | need | directions? |
| | they | | |
| Does | he | | |
| | she | | |
| | it | | |

| Short answers | | | | | | |
|---|---|---|---|---|---|---|
| Yes, | you | do. | No, | you | don't. |
| | we | | | we | |
| | I | | | I | |
| | they | | | they | |
| | he | does. | | he | doesn't. |
| | she | | | she | |
| | it | | | it | |

**E.** Complete the conversations. Use the simple present tense.

1. **A:** Excuse me. _*Do you have*_____ this shirt in small?
   you / have

   **B:** Yes, we _____. This way, please.

2. **A:** _____ a uniform?
   Julia / need

   **B:** Yes, she _____. She needs size 6.

3. **A:** _____ large shirts?
   they / want

   **B:** No, they _____. They want medium.

4. **A:** _____ his receipt?
   customer / have

   **B:** No, he _____.

| Question word | do / does | Subject | Base form of the verb |
|---|---|---|---|
| **What** color | **do** | you | **want?** |
| **What** size | **does** | he | **need?** |
| **What** | **does** | she | **have?** |

| Answers |
|---|
| Blue, please. |
| He needs size 12. |
| She has the receipt. |

**F.** Put the words in order. Write the information questions with **do** or **does**.

1. **A:** _What size do you need?_        **B:** Size 10, please.
   you / What size / need

2. **A:** _____?        **B:** She likes green.
   like / What color / she

3. **A:** _____?        **B:** New uniforms for work.
   they / need / What

4. **A:** _____?        **B:** She needs large.
   need / she / What size

5. **A:** _____?        **B:** Black pants in size 36.
   What / he / want

6. **A:** _____?        **B:** They have a receipt.
   have / they / What / do

## 6. This, that, these, and those

**G.** **Look at the pictures.  Complete the sentences.  Write <u>this</u>, <u>that</u>, <u>these</u>, or <u>those</u>.**

1. I don't like <u>these</u> shoes.

2. I want _____ pants.

3. Do you like _____ dress?

4. I don't like _____ tie.

# U N I T   5

## 1. <u>It's</u> for days, dates, and times

| Days | A: **Is it** Tuesday or Wednesday?   B: **It's** Wednesday. |
|------|------------------------------------------------------------|
| Dates | **It's** September 21, 2004. |
| Times | A: **Is it** 5:00?   B: No, **it isn't. It's** 4:45. |

**A.** Look at the pictures. Write the answers to the questions.

1. Is it Saturday?    No, it isn't.
2. What day is it?    _____
3. Is it November?    _____
4. What month is it?  _____
5. What year is it?   _____
6. Is it midnight?    _____
7. What time is it?   _____

## 2. In, on, at, from, and to for telling time

| in + month | School starts **in** September. |
| | It ends **in** June. |
| on + day | We have class **on** Monday. |
| | We don't have class **on** July 4. |
| at + time | The post office opens **at** 9:00. |
| | It closes **at** 5:00. |
| from ____ to ____ | School is open **from** September **to** June. |
| (months, days, times) | He works **from** Monday **to** Friday. |
| | We have class **from** 9:00 **to** 10:30. |

**Things to remember**

The bank **opens** at 9:00 and **closes** at 3:00.

The bank **is open** from 9:00 to 3:00.

**B.** Write in, on, at, or from . . . to.

1. School ends __in__ June.
2. That store opens _____ 9:00 a.m.
3. I don't have class _____ Saturday or Sunday.
4. I work _____ 8:30 _____ 4:30.
5. He is in the restaurant _____ noon.
6. We don't have school _____ July.
7. Schools aren't open _____ January 1.
8. The office is closed _____ 12:00 _____ 1:00 p.m.

| What time | is it? | It's 2:15. |
|---|---|---|
| What time | is the class? | At 11:00. |
| When | does the restaurant open? | |
| When | is the bank open? | From 9:00 to 5:00. |

**C.** **Choose words. Write the words on the line.**

1. **A:** What time ____is____ it?
   is / does

   **B:** 4:30.

2. **A:** What time _____ the post office close?
   is / does

   **B:** At 5:00.

3. **A:** _____ is that store open?
   When / What

   **B:** From 9:00 a.m. to 9:00 p.m.

4. **A:** _____ time does your class start?
   When / What

   **B:** At 8:00 a.m.

5. **A:** When _____ your English class?
   is / does

   **B:** On Monday and Wednesday.

6. **A:** What time _____ the class start?
   is / does

   **B:** At 5:30 p.m.

**D.** **Look at the pictures. Put the words in order to make a question. Write the answers to the questions.**

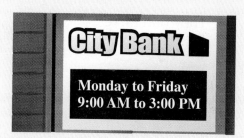

1. **A:** _When is the supermarket open?_
   the / is / open / When / supermarket

   **B:** _____

2. **A:** _____?
   When / the / supermarket / open / does

   **B:** _____

3. **A:** _____?
   close / does / the / What time / bank

   **B:** _____

4. **A:** _____?
   When / the / bank / open / is

   **B:** _____

# UNIT 6

## 1. Count nouns and non-count nouns

| COUNT NOUNS | | NON-COUNT NOUNS |
|---|---|---|
| Singular | Plural | |
| a carrot | carrots | water |
| an onion | onions | rice |

**A.** Look at the pictures. Complete the sentences.

1. He doesn't like
   __fish__.

2. He has
   __a tomato__.

3. You need a bag of
   _____.

4. They don't like
   _____.

5. Do you like
   _____?

6. We need two bottles
   of _____.

7. Do you want
   _____?

8. They like
   _____.

## 2. Questions with <u>How many</u> and <u>How much</u>

| How many | Count noun | |
|---|---|---|
| How many | apples | do we need? |
| | boxes of rice | |

| How much | Non-count noun | |
|---|---|---|
| How much | apple juice | do we need? |
| | rice | |

**B.** Complete the questions with <u>How many</u> or <u>How much</u>.

1. _How much_____ bread do we have?

2. _____ bottles of juice are on the shelf?

3. _____ meat do you eat?

4. _____ eggs do you eat in a week?

5. _____ bags of onions are there?

6. _____ coffee does he drink at work?

## 3. There is and There are

| There is | Singular noun | |
|---|---|---|
| There is | a bottle of milk | in the refrigerator. |
| (There's) | an egg | |

| There is | Non-count noun | |
|---|---|---|
| There is | juice | in the refrigerator. |
| (There's) | milk | |

| There are | Plural noun | |
|---|---|---|
| There are | two bottles of milk | in the refrigerator. |
| | apples | |

### C. Write There's or There are.

1. _There's_ a supermarket on Park Street.

2. _There are_ two restaurants on Elm Street.

3. _____ sugar in the tea.

4. _____ rice in those boxes.

5. _____ six eggs in the refrigerator.

6. _____ supplies on the shelves.

7. _____ coffee in that can.

8. _____ an onion in this bag.

## 4. Is there any and Are there any: yes / no questions

| Is there any | Non-count noun | |
|---|---|---|
| Is there any | rice | on the shelf? |
| | coffee | |

| Short answers | |
|---|---|
| Yes, there is. | No, there isn't. |

| Are there any | Plural noun | |
|---|---|---|
| Are there any | boxes of rice | on the shelf? |
| | onions | |

| Short answers | |
|---|---|
| Yes, there are. | No, there aren't. |

**D.** Complete the conversations with <u>Is there any</u> and <u>Are there any</u>.  Write the short answers.

1.  A: <u>Is there any milk in the refrigerator?</u>
    milk / in the refrigerator
    B: Yes, _____ there is _____.

2.  A: _____ ?
    people / in the restaurant
    B: Yes, _____.

3.  A: _____ ?
    sugar / in this coffee
    B: No, _____.

4.  A: _____ ?
    cans of beans / on the shelf
    B: No, _____.

**E.** Look at the picture.  Write questions with <u>Is there any</u> or <u>Are there any</u> . . . <u>on the shelf</u>.
Write answers.

1.  A: <u>Is there any apple juice on the shelf?</u>
    apple juice
    B: <u>Yes, there is. There are two bottles of apple juice.</u>

2.  A: _____ ?
    cans of coffee
    B: _____

3.  A: _____ ?
    tea
    B: _____

4.  A: _____ ?
    bread
    B: _____

5.  A: _____ ?
    onions
    B: _____

6.  A: _____ ?
    tomatoes
    B: _____

## 1. The present continuous: statements

| Subject | be | Verb + -ing |
|---------|-----|-------------|
| I | am | |
| We<br>You<br>They | are | working. |
| He<br>She<br>It | is | |

| Subject | be | not | Verb + -ing |
|---------|-----|-----|-------------|
| I | am | | |
| We<br>You<br>They | are | not | working. |
| He<br>She<br>It | is | | |

**Things to remember**
1. Present continuous verbs have two parts: (1) <u>am</u>, <u>is</u>, or <u>are</u> and (2) verb + <u>-ing</u>.
2. Verbs that end in <u>-e</u> drop the <u>-e</u> and add <u>-ing</u>:
   drive   driving   come   coming
3. You can use contractions with <u>be</u>:
   **I'm** reading.  They **aren't** talking.

**A.** Complete the sentences with the present continuous. Use the words <u>clean</u>, <u>fix</u>, <u>read</u>, and <u>write</u>.

1. _He's fixing_____

   his car.

2. _____

   a book.

3. _____

   the restroom.

4. _____

   her name.

**B.** Complete each negative sentence with the present continuous. Use contractions.

1. Juan is at home. _He isn't working_____ now.
   he / not / work

2. I'm looking at this book. _____ the newspaper.
   I / not / read

3. We're out of rice. _____ rice today.
   we / not / eat

4. Anna is in Room 24 now. _____ Room 26.
   she / not / clean

5. The mechanic is on the phone. _____ my car now.
   he / not / fix

6. You're studying English. _____ now.
   you / not / cook

## 2. The present continuous: yes / no questions and short answers

| Be | Subject | Verb + -ing |
|---|---|---|
| Am | I | |
| Are | we<br>you<br>they | helping? |
| Is | he<br>she<br>it | |

| Short answers | | | | | | |
|---|---|---|---|---|---|---|
| Yes, | you<br>we<br>you<br>they | are. | No, | you<br>we<br>you<br>they | aren't. |
| | he<br>she<br>it | is. | | he<br>she<br>it | isn't. |

**C.** Complete the conversations. Use the present continuous.

1. **A:** <u>Are you eating</u> now?
   you / eat
   **B:** Yes, we _____ are _____.

2. **A:** _____ supplies?
   George / buy
   **B:** Yes, he _____.

3. **A:** _____ coffee?
   you / drink
   **B:** No, I _____. This is tea.

4. **A:** _____ to school?
   your daughters / go
   **B:** No, they _____.
   They are sick today.

5. **A:** _____ the computer?
   Ana / fix
   **B:** No, she _____. Irina is.

## 3. The present continuous: information questions

| Question word | be | Subject | Verb + -ing | |
|---|---|---|---|---|
| What | are | you | doing? | |
| Where | is | he | going? | |
| Who | is | | cleaning | Room 12? |

| Answers |
|---|
| I'm cooking rice. |
| To work. |
| Marta is. |

**D.** Write information questions in the present continuous.

1. **A:** <u>What's Ms. Wang doing?</u>
   what / Ms. Wang / do
   **B:** She's studying.

2. **A:** _____?
   where / you / go
   **B:** To the store. We need milk.

3. **A:** _____?
   who / talk / to the manager
   **B:** Mr. Duval is.

4. **A:** _____?
   what / you / buy
   **B:** Cleaning supplies.

5. **A:** _____?
   who / fix / your car
   **B:** My brother.

| Subject | can / can't | Base form of the verb |
|---------|-------------|----------------------|
| I<br>We<br>You<br>They<br>He<br>She<br>It | **can**<br><br>**can't** | **start.** |

| Contraction |
|-------------|
| can + not = **can't** |

**Things to remember**

Be careful! Don't use <u>to</u> after <u>can</u>.

She can fix cars.
NOT She can to fix cars.

**E.** **Look at the chart. What can Rafael and Luisa do? Write sentences with <u>can</u> or <u>can't</u>.**

|  | Rafael | Luisa |
|--|--------|-------|
| cook | no | yes |
| drive a bus | yes | no |
| fix cars | yes | no |

1. He _____ *can't cook.* _____
2. He _____
3. He _____

4. She _____ *can cook.* _____
5. She _____
6. She _____

## 5. <u>Can</u>: <u>yes</u> / <u>no</u> questions and short answers

| <u>Can</u> | Subject | Base form of the verb | |
|------------|---------|----------------------|--|
| **Can** | you<br>they<br>Mr. Lee | **fix** | cars? |

| Short answers | | | | | | |
|---------------|---|---|---|---|---|---|
| Yes, | I<br>they<br>he | **can.** | No, | I<br>they<br>he | **can't.** |

**F.** **Complete the conversations with <u>can</u>.**

1. **A:** *Can you fix computers?* _____
   you / fix computers
   **B:** No, _____.

2. **A:** _____?
   Angela / answer the phone
   **B:** No, _____.

3. **A:** _____?
   you / come to class tomorrow
   **B:** Yes, _____.

4. **A:** _____?
   they / clean the office now
   **B:** No, _____.

5. **A:** _____?
   he / cook spaghetti
   **B:** Yes, _____.

## 6. Can: information questions

| Question word | can | Subject | Base form of the verb | | Answers |
|---|---|---|---|---|---|
| What | | she | do? | | She can drive a bus. |
| When | can | we | go | home? | In 15 minutes. |
| Where | | I | buy | a cup of coffee? | At the store on the corner. |
| Who | | | fix | the lawn mower? | Mr. Rogers can. |

**G.** Put the words in order. Write information questions. Complete the answers.

1. **A:** _What can Lisa do?_____
       do / Lisa / What / can

   **B:** She _____ _can_ _____ fix cars.

2. **A:** _____?
       Anton / What / drive / can

   **B:** He _____ drive a bus.

3. **A:** _____?
       rice and beans / Who / can / cook

   **B:** Li _____ cook rice and beans.

4. **A:** _____?
       Mark / Where / work / can

   **B:** He _____ work in a school.

## 7. Have to: statements

| Subject | have to / has to | Base form of the verb | |
|---|---|---|---|
| I | have to | go | to school. |
| He | has to | | |

| Subject | don't / doesn't | have to | Base form of the verb | |
|---|---|---|---|---|
| They | don't | have to | go | to school. |
| She | doesn't | | | |

**H.** Complete each sentence. Use a form of **have to** and the verb.

1. You _____ _don't have to come_ _____ to work on Monday.
            not / come

2. The electrician _____ a new telephone.
                        install

3. We _____ the supply room in an hour.
           clean

4. Nadia _____ on the bus. She can drive.
              not go

5. Esteban and I _____ tonight. Do you?
                      not study

GB-20    Grammar Booster

## 8. Have to: yes / no questions and short answers

| Do / Does | Subject | have to | Base form of the verb | |
|---|---|---|---|---|
| **Do** | you | **have to** | **stay** | home? |
| **Does** | Lucy | | | |

| Short answers |
|---|
| Yes, I **do**. <br> No, I **don't**. |
| Yes, she **does**. <br> No, she **doesn't**. |

**I.** Complete the conversations with <u>have to</u> and short answers.

1. **A:** *Do you have to go to the bank?*
   <br>                   you / go to the bank

   **B:** No, _____ *I don't.* _____

2. **A:** _____?
   <br>                   we / buy eggs

   **B:** Yes, _____.

3. **A:** _____?
   <br>               Ms. Rios / work today

   **B:** No, _____.

4. **A:** _____?
   <br>              he / fix the lawn mower

   **B:** Yes, _____.

## 9. Have to: information questions

| Question word | do / does | Subject | have to | Base form of the verb | |
|---|---|---|---|---|---|
| **Why** | **do** | I | **have to** | **go** | to the store? |
| **What** | **does** | Dan | | **do?** | |
| **Who** | | | **has to** | **clean** | the stove? |

| Answers |
|---|
| Because we're out of milk. |
| He has to talk to the manager. |
| I do. Gina and I do. |

**J.** Read the conversations. Complete the questions.

1. **A:** The manager can't talk to you now. You have to come back at 3:00.

   **B:** Excuse me? What time _____ *do I have to come back?* _____

2. **A:** We don't have any sugar. You have to go to the supply room.

   **B:** Excuse me? Where _____?

3. **A:** Your son has to take this medicine.

   **B:** Excuse me? What _____?

4. **A:** Lana doesn't have to clean the shelves. Gloria has to do it.

   **B:** Excuse me? Who _____?

# UNIT 8

## 1. Possessives

| Subject pronoun | Possessive | Subject Pronoun | Possessive |
|---|---|---|---|
| I | **my** | we | **our** |
| you | **your** | you | **your** |
| he | **his** | they | **their** |
| she | **her** | | |
| it | **its** | | |

| Noun | Possessive |
|---|---|
| Juan | Juan's |
| doctor | doctor's |

**Things to remember**
Use a possessive before a noun, like <u>name</u>, <u>doctor</u>, and <u>friends</u>.
**My name** is Phuong.
Who's **your doctor**?
They're **Clara's friends**.

**A.** **Complete the sentences. Use possessives.**

1. I have to make a doctor's appointment. I hurt ___my___ neck.

2. Ms. Nguyen hurt _____ back. She can't work today.

3. Can I call you back? What's _____ phone number?

4. Mona and Charles aren't at home today. _____ father is in the hospital.

5. Dan has a cold. _____ mother is making chicken soup.

6. We can't call the doctor. _____ phone isn't working.

**B.** **Look at the family tree. Complete the sentences. Use possessives.**

1. William is _____Anna's_____ husband.

2. Anna is _____ wife.

3. Nadia is _____ sister.

4. Denzell is _____ brother.

**C.** **Look at the family tree. Complete the conversations.
Use possessives.**

1. **A:** Nadia, what is your _____brother's_____ name?
   **B:** Denzell.

2. **A:** Anna, what is your _____ name?
   **B:** William.

3. **A:** Denzell, what is your _____ name?
   **B:** Anna.

4. **A:** William, what is your _____ name?
   **B:** Nadia.

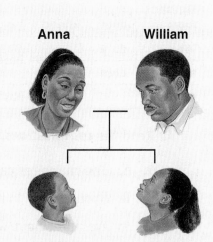

**Anna**        **William**

**Denzell**        **Nadia**

**A FAMILY TREE**

## 2. Their, there, and they're

| Their / there / they're |
| --- |
| **Their house** is white. |
| **There** are apples on the table. |
| **They're** fixing my car. |

**Things to remember**

_Their_ is a possessive. Use _their_ before a noun.

Use _there_ with _is_ or _are_.

_They're_ is the contraction for _they are_.

**D.** **Choose words. Write the words on the line.**

1. Mr. and Mrs. Ivanov have a son. _Their_____ son's name is Tima.
   <br>There / Their

2. _____ are three people in the family.
   <br>There / They're

3. _____ from Russia.
   <br>Their / They're

4. Mr. and Mrs. Ivanov are at school. _____ going to class now.
   <br>There / They're

5. _____ school is on High Street.
   <br>They're / Their

6. Are _____ any stores on High Street?
   <br>there / their

## 3. Never, sometimes, and always in statements

| Subject | never / sometimes / always | Simple present tense verb | |
| --- | --- | --- | --- |
| He | **never** | **goes** | to the doctor. |
| My back | **sometimes** | **hurts.** | |
| I | **always** | **take** | aspirin. |

| Subject | be | never / sometimes / always | |
| --- | --- | --- | --- |
| I | **am** | **never** | ready on time. |
| She | **is** | **sometimes** | late. |
| You | **are** | **always** | busy. |

**E.** **Put the words in order. Write the sentences.**

1. never / Mr. Leu / has / headaches   _Mr. Leu never has headaches._____

2. on time / is / She / always   _____

3. They / drive / to school / sometimes   _____

4. go / to the emergency room / never / I   _____

5. Carmen's back / hurts / always   _____

6. sometimes / am / I / sick   _____

|  | Present continuous | Simple present tense |
|---|---|---|
|  | He's **calling** the doctor now. | He **always calls** the doctor when he has a fever. |
|  | She's **working** today. | She **never stays** home when she has a cold. |

**F.** Complete the sentences with the correct form of the verb.

1. She _____is taking_____ her medicine now.
   takes / is taking

2. The doctor always _____ late.
   works / is working

3. He _____ a fever.
   doesn't have / isn't having

4. He _____ an ambulance.
   needs / is needing

5. They _____ to the teacher now.
   talk / are talking

6. You always _____ to work.
   drive / are driving

**G.** Write the present continuous or the simple present tense of the verb.

1. My son _____has_____ the flu.
   have

2. Listen! A fire truck _____.
   come

3. He never _____ tea in the morning.
   drink

4. You _____ the doctor now.
   call

5. My ankle sometimes _____.
   hurt

6. I always _____ this medicine when I have a cold.
   take

## 1. Be going to:  statements

| Subject | be | (not) | going to | Base form of the verb |
|---|---|---|---|---|
| I | am | | | |
| We<br>You<br>They | are | (not) | going to | leave. |
| He<br>She<br>It | is | | | |

**Things to remember**

You can use contractions with the verb be:

They **aren't** going to buy a car tomorrow.

**A.** Write sentences.  Use a form of **be going to**.

1. he / cash his paycheck     *He's going to cash his paycheck.* _____

2. I / not / go shopping     _____

3. she / send money home     _____

4. he / not / pay those bills     _____

5. these shoes / be on sale soon     _____

## 2. Be going to:  yes / no questions and short answers

| Be | Subject | going to | Base form of the verb | |
|---|---|---|---|---|
| Am | I | | | |
| Are | you<br>they | going to | need | cash? |
| Is | she<br>he | | | |

**Short answers**

| | | | | | | |
|---|---|---|---|---|---|---|
| | you | are. | | you | aren't. |
| Yes, | we<br>they | are. | No, | we<br>they | aren't. |
| | she<br>he | is. | | she<br>he | isn't. |

**B.** Complete the **yes / no** questions about the future.  Use a form of **be going to**.  Complete the short answers.

1. **A:** *Are you going to go* shopping on Saturday?    **B:** No, we _____.
   <br>      you / go

2. **A:** _____ cash?    **B:** Yes, they _____.
   <br>      they / pay

3. **A:** _____ an ambulance?    **B:** No, he _____.
   <br>      that man / need

4. **A:** _____ to the bank?    **B:** Yes, she _____.
   <br>      she / go

## 3. Be going to: information questions

| Question word | be | Subject | going to | Base form of the verb | | Answers |
|---|---|---|---|---|---|---|
| **What** | **are** | you | | **do** | tonight? | I'm going to stay home. |
| **When** | **is** | Martin | **going to** | **buy** | a car? | In a few days. |
| **Who** | **is** | | | **go** | to the bank? | Angela. |

**C.** Write questions with be going to. Choose the answer from the box.

> At 11:00.      Go to a movie.      In two weeks.      My father is.

1. **A:** what / you / do / tonight *What are you going to do tonight?* _____
   **B:** _____

2. **A:** when / you / get your first paycheck _____?
   **B:** _____

3. **A:** who / pay the bills _____?
   **B:** _____

4. **A:** what time / you / go to bed _____?
   **B:** _____

## 4. Questions with Whose

| Whose | Noun | | Answers |
|---|---|---|---|
| **Whose** | money | is this? | That's my money. |
| | quarters | are these? | Those are my quarters. |

**D.** Write a question with Whose about each thing. Write the answers.

**Anna and William Lee**

1. *Whose tie is it?* _____     *It's William's tie.* _____

2. _____     _____

3. _____     _____

4. _____     _____

## 5. Review of question words

| Question words | | Answers |
|---|---|---|
| **What** | do you do? | I'm a cashier. |
| **Who** | are they? | They're Mr. and Mrs. Park. |
| **Where** | is the restroom? | Down the hall, on the left. |
| **When** | do you have to start? | Next Monday. |
| **Why** | is she calling the doctor? | She hurt her back. |
| **How** **much** money | does he have? | $100. |
| **many** bills | | Four or five. |

**E.** **Write an information question for each answer.**

1. **A:** I can't go to the movies tonight.

   **B:** _Why can't you go to the movies?_ _____

   **A:** Because I don't have any money!

2. **A:** Maria is cooking tonight.

   **B:** _____?

   **A:** Chicken and rice.

3. **A:** I'm going to call Ms. Gomez.

   **B:** _____?

   **A:** She's the manager.

4. **A:** I'm returning this microwave.

   **B:** _____?

   **A:** Because it's too large.

5. **A:** They're going to buy a car.

   **B:** _____?

   **A:** Next week.

6. **A:** She has a lot of credit cards.

   **B:** _____?

   **A:** Seven or eight.

7. **A:** We always go food shopping on Saturday morning.

   **B:** _____?

   **A:** At the Union Supermarket on High Street.

## 1. The past tense of the verb be:  statements

| AFFIRMATIVE | | |
|---|---|---|
| **Subject** | **be** | |
| I He She It | **was** | at school yesterday. |
| We You They | **were** | |

| NEGATIVE | | |
|---|---|---|
| **Subject** | **be** | |
| I He She It | **wasn't** | at school last week. |
| We You They | **weren't** | |

| Contractions |
|---|
| was + not = **wasn't** |
| were + not = **weren't** |

**A.**  Write <u>was</u>, <u>wasn't</u>, <u>were</u>, or <u>weren't</u>.

1.  Vi ___*was*___ a mechanic in his country, but now he's a truck driver.

2.  This is his first class at this school.  He _____ here last year.

3.  Inessa and Oksana _____ cashiers, but now they're managers.

4.  You _____ in school yesterday.  Why not? _____ you sick?

5.  I _____ on time for my interview yesterday.  I _____ happy.

## 2. The past tense of the verb be:  <u>yes</u> / <u>no</u> questions

| **Be** | **Subject** | |
|---|---|---|
| **Was** | I | late? |
| | he it | |
| **Were** | you they | |

| Short answers | | | | | |
|---|---|---|---|---|---|
| Yes, | you | **were.** | No, | you | **weren't.** |
| | he it | **was.** | | he it | **wasn't.** |
| | we they | **were.** | | we they | **weren't.** |

**B.** Look at the pictures. Write <u>yes/no</u> questions with <u>was</u> and <u>were</u>. Write the short answers.

1. **A:** <u>Was Vanessa a doctor</u> in 2001?
              doctor

   **B:** <u>Yes, she was</u> .

**Vanessa in 2001**

2. **A:** _____ last year?
             a plumber

   **B:** _____. He was a firefighter.

**Leo last year**

3. **A:** _____ in 1990?
             a writer

   **B:** _____. She was a teacher.

**Ms. Hall in 1990**

## 3. The past tense of the verb <u>be</u>: information questions

| Question word | <u>be</u> | Subject | |
|---|---|---|---|
| **What** | **was** | his last job? | |
| **How long** | **were** | you | at the hospital? |
| **Who** | **was** | | on the phone? |

| Answers |
|---|
| He was a sanitation worker. |
| From 9:00 to 12:30. |
| Ms. Chen. |

**C.** Write questions with <u>was</u> and <u>were</u>.

1. **A:** <u>Where were you in 2002?</u>
           where / you / in 2002

   **B:** In China.

2. **A:** _____?
           how long / he / a dishwasher

   **B:** For a year. Now he's a cashier.

3. **A:** _____?
           when / your interview

   **B:** Yesterday.

4. **A:** _____?
           who / your manager / at that job

   **B:** Ms. Esposito.

## 4. Simple past tense statements with regular verbs

| Subject | Past tense form of the verb | |
|---|---|---|
| I<br>We<br>You<br>They<br>He<br>She<br>It | worked | for two years. |

| Subject | didn't | Base form of the verb | |
|---|---|---|---|
| I<br>We<br>You<br>They<br>He<br>She<br>It | didn't | work | for two years. |

**Things to remember**

Use the base form of the verb after <u>didn't</u>.

**D.** **Complete the sentences with the simple past tense.**

1. I ___*didn't use*___ the cash register.
       not use

2. The sink is out of order. The plumber _____ it.
                                               not fix

3. Last week, we _____ our new telephones.
                      install

4. I _____ the lawn mower to cut the grass on Saturday.
        use

5. The dishwashers _____ all the dishes yesterday.
                        not wash

6. A receptionist _____ the visitors at the front desk.
                       greet

7. Two aides _____ the nurses yesterday.
                  help

8. We want to paint our house this year. We _____ it last year.
                                                 not paint

## 5. Simple past tense statements with irregular verbs

| Subject | Past tense | |
|---|---|---|
| He | sold | children's clothes. |

| Subject | didn't | Base form of the verb | |
|---|---|---|---|
| He | didn't | sell | children's clothes. |

**E.** **Complete the sentences. Write the simple past tense of the verb.**

1. He was a truck driver. He _____*drove*_____ a truck for ten years.
   drive

2. Max _____ his car yet.
   not sell

3. Ms. Durosier was late, so she _____ the bus.
   not take

4. Elena hurt her back, but she _____ any aspirin.
   not take

5. A hairdresser at Broadway Hair _____ my hair. Do you like it?
   cut

## 6. The simple past tense: <u>yes</u> / <u>no</u> questions

| <u>Did</u> | Subject | Base form of the verb |
|---|---|---|
| **Did** | I<br>they<br>she | **help?** |

| Short answers | | | | | |
|---|---|---|---|---|---|
| Yes, | you<br>they<br>she | **did.** | No, | you<br>they<br>she | **didn't.** |

**F.** **Complete the <u>yes</u> / <u>no</u> questions and short answers. Use the simple past tense.**

1. **A:** I was a plumber for five years.

   **B:** *Did you install* _____ sinks and toilets?
   you / install

   **A:** Yes, _____.

2. **A:** I was a hairdresser for two years.

   **B:** _____ children's hair?
   you / cut

   **A:** No, _____.

3. **A:** My wife was a child care worker in our country.

   **B:** _____ at a child care center?
   she / work

   **A:** Yes, _____.

4. **A:** My father worked for the telephone company from 1960 to 2002.

   **B:** _____ telephones?
   he / fix

   **A:** No, _____. He was a salesperson.

5. **A:** My friends were teachers for many years.

   **B:** _____ English?
   they / teach

   **A:** Yes, _____.

| Question word | did | Subject | Base form of the verb | |
|---|---|---|---|---|
| What | | you | do | at your last job? |
| How long | did | he | work | at the hospital? |
| When | | they | sell | their house? |

| Answers |
|---|
| I installed telephones. |
| For a year. |
| They sold it last month. |

| Who | Simple past verb | |
|---|---|---|
| Who | fixed | the phones? |
| | cut | your hair? |

| Answers |
|---|
| A telephone technician. |
| My sister did. She always cuts it for me. |

**G.** Complete the questions about the past. Use <u>Who</u>, <u>What</u>, <u>How long</u>, <u>How many</u>, or <u>Where</u>.

1. **A:** _What did you do_ _____ in your country?

   **B:** I was a homemaker. I took care of my family.

2. **A:** _____ trucks?

   **B:** I drove trucks for seventeen years.

3. **A:** _____ rooms _____?

   **B:** They painted three: two meeting rooms and one supply room.

4. **A:** _____ the man to the hospital?

   **B:** The paramedics did. They took him in the ambulance.

5. **A:** _____ care of your children when you were at work?

   **B:** My sister did.

6. **A:** _____ at her last job?

   **B:** She was a nurse.

   **A:** _____?

   **B:** She worked in a hospital emergency room.

   **A:** _____ at that hospital?

   **B:** From 2001 to last year.